The story of the sandy-haired boy who went to Reverend Marye's school, the young surveyor, the burgess in colonial Williamsburg, the commander-in-chief of the army during the American Revolution, the first president of the United States.

George Washington *Leader of the People*

Illustrated by ROBERT FRANKENBERG

George Washington

Leader of the People

Clara Ingram Judson

FOLLETT PUBLISHING COMPANY Chicago

Books by Clara Ingram Judson

Abraham Lincoln, Friend of the People
Andrew Carnegie
Andrew Jackson, Frontier Statesman
Benjamin Franklin
Bruce Carries the Flag
Christopher Columbus was a Sailor (1964)
George Washington, Leader of the People
The Lost Violin
Michael's Victory
The Mighty Soo
Mr. Justice Holmes
Petar's Treasure
Pierre's Lucky Pouch
Reaper Man, The Story of Cyrus Hall McCormick
St. Lawrence Seaway
Sod-House Winter
Theodore Roosevelt, Fighting Patriot
Thomas Jefferson, Champion of the People

For Younger Readers

Abraham Lincoln
Christopher Columbus
George Washington

Library of Congress Catalog Card Number: 51-14416

Author's Foreword

This story of George Washington begins at the scene of his remembered boyhood, Ferry farm, in Virginia. Parson Weems, Washington's first biographer, chose this same farm for his popular fictions, and it has been a challenge to separate truth from fancy and to write with fidelity of the busy farm life by the Rappahannock.

Washington, more than most of our national heroes, has suffered from the good intentions of his early biographers. The fashion in writing of their time required that a hero be perfect, free of human frailties, almost a prig. Earnest debunkers, writing at the other extreme a century later, did little to acquaint us with the real man.

Modern scholarly research has brought to light long-neglected documents; and studies at Mount Vernon and Williamsburg, Virginia, have revealed a true account of buildings, farms, friends, loves, and labors. It becomes possible, now, to get a real understanding of our first president as farmer, soldier, statesman, and citizen.

After my long study of books and documents, my daughter Mary Jane and I took a leisurely journey through the Washington country. As we lingered in scenes that he loved, a clearer knowledge of the man unfolded; a man who was moved by natural beauty and liked to help things grow; one who rode, danced, and visited his neighbors, who was kind and generous to those who needed him. As we knew General Washington better, we could appreciate the deep sacrifices he made when, three times, he left these cherished scenes to serve his country.

Later, as the writing progressed, I found the straight narrative form quite inadequate to depict the vigorous, friendly man I had come to know. So the book contains many dramatized scenes, which, however, are historically accurate. Where possible, I have used actual words spoken. Where no records are available, I have used words and phrases from letters, diaries, and newspapers of the time.

In the long study preceding the writing of this biography, I had generous help from many people and books. Among these I wish especially to thank:

Mr. Worth Bailey, Research Associate, The Mount Vernon Ladies Association of the Union, Mount Vernon, Virginia, who made valuable suggestions for research and read my manuscript; my daughter Mary Jane (Mrs. Kingsley L. Rice), who was my driver-companion on the fact-seeking tour of the Washington country; Mr. Douglas Southall Freeman, whose two-volume *Young Washington* was an inspiration.

Mr. John Melville Jennings, Librarian, Virginia Historical Society, Richmond, Virginia; Mr. George H. Fairchild, Historian, Historical Society of Pennsylvania, Philadelphia, Pennsylvania; Miss Harriet Swift, Curator of Americana, Boston Public Library, Boston, Massachusetts.

The Evanston Public Library, and particularly Miss Louise Borchelt and Miss Florence Davison; Deering Library, Northwestern University, Evanston, Illinois, and Miss Helen Perkins of the staff; and several members of the staff of Colonial Williamsburg, Williamsburg, Virginia.

C. I. J.

Evanston, Illinois
August 7, 1951

A Note on this Biography

George Washington loved children and customarily presented to "the little ones" of whom he was fond the best books for juvenile readers that the eighteenth century could supply. Happily, children's books have progressed a long way from the maxim and chapbook stage and the folklore moralizing of the nineteenth century by men like Weems, of cherry-tree fame. I believe the General himself would approve of *George Washington, Leader of the People,* the biography which Mrs. Judson has written especially for the young, with a complete understanding of Washington's time and a thorough regard for historic truth. She has portrayed simply and straightforwardly the character of the hero, rekindling with suspense and drama the highlights and accomplishments of his life. What a message for young America to read!

WORTH BAILEY
Research Associate
The Mount Vernon Ladies Association
of the Union

George Washington *Leader of the People*

By the Rappahannock

The farm by the river was the lush green of June in Virginia. The air was warm, fine for growing things. A mocking bird sang in the linden tree and the chatter of wrens mingled with domestic noises of roosters, hens, and ducks in the chicken yard.

A house, high above the Rappahannock, had a comfortable look against a line of tall trees. Nearby, a barn, the kitchen, poultry house, storeroom, smithy and quarters for the slaves made a little settlement such as was usually found on prosperous Virginia farms in that year 1739.

At the horse lot a boy tugged at the heavy gate bar, while his pony, Whitefoot, pawed impatiently, eager to be gone.

"Want help?" Tim, the stableman, called.

"No, I can do it myself," George Washington said quickly. As he tugged again, he noticed that Whitefoot was suddenly still, ears cocked as though he heard a new sound.

"Someone coming, Whitefoot?" George asked, listening. The rhythmic sound of hoofbeats came from far down the lane leading to the main road to Fredericksburg.

George climbed onto the fence for a look. He was sturdy and tall for a boy in his eighth year. Freckles sprinkled his

straight nose, and his hands were tanned from long hours out
of doors. Now he brushed a lock of sandy-colored hair from
his forehead and squinted his gray-blue eyes down the lane.

"It's *Lawrence!*" he cried excitedly. "Whitefoot! Lawrence is coming!"

George jumped down from the fence, pulled out the gate
bar, which suddenly seemed lighter, threw himself onto his
pony and dashed off down the lane.

A visit from George's twenty-one-year-old half-brother was
a thrilling surprise. Lawrence Washington had been home
from England only a few months. George admired this tall,
handsome brother and saw him far too little.

Lawrence waved as George drew near and grinned with
amusement when the boy pulled Whitefoot up short with a
flourish that sent pebbles flying.

"Oh, Lawrence! I am so glad to see you!" George cried
breathlessly. "I didn't know you were coming today!"

"I started early; I have meant to come for several days,"
Lawrence said. "Is Father here?"

"No," George told him. "I think he is at the iron works.
Maybe you had better ride over and see him?"

"No, my errand is here," Lawrence said. "And I doubt if
your mother would let you ride over with me in any case.
Where are you bound now?"

"To school," George told him in a bored tone. "That
Master Hobby is a tiresome man, Lawrence. He teaches the
same thing over and over."

"Perhaps it is a good thing that I came today," Lawrence remarked as they rode along toward the house.

"Did you come about *me?*" George was astonished. But Lawrence merely shook his head and laughed mysteriously.

"I must talk to your mother now," he said. "And you should shut that gate, George. You will be in trouble if a colt gets into the field."

Reluctantly George stopped to close and fasten the gate while Lawrence rode to the hitching post near the house.

George turned Whitefoot into the lot, fastened the gate and called to a stableboy to care for Lawrence's mount. But his manner was absent-minded; his thoughts were on Lawrence. Something was up, that was certain, something that concerned George. But what could be important enough to bring Lawrence on a thirty-mile ride from Hunting Creek farm? In June, too, when a farmer had work to oversee.

Shouts of small children and the bark of a dog guided George to the lawn in front of the house. There, on the high bank Lawrence had joined Mrs. Washington and the younger children, Betty, Sam, and Jack. They had been watching their father's scow as it crossed the river.

"It is a good thing you came today, Lawrence," Mrs. Washington was saying to her stepson as George came near. "While you are in Fredericksburg about George, you can attend to the delivery of my boxes. I saw the ship from England arrive yesterday."

"Am I going to Fredericksburg?" George exclaimed.

Many times he had looked toward the white steeple of the church across the river and wondered what was beneath the thick trees. "I have never been to a town," he added.

"That is not surprising," Lawrence said casually. "Virginia has few towns. But you shall see Fredericksburg today, for my errand there is for you. Father thinks it is high time. . ."

"George! Run to the house and put on your best coat," Mrs. Washington interrupted. "Lawrence can explain your father's plan while you are on the ferry. It comes now." The scow had reached the landing at the foot of the ravine.

George glanced down at his shirt and kneepants. The garments were clean and good enough for Hobby's little school. But he did look shabby compared with Lawrence's elegant coat and breeches, trimmed with shining buttons and buckles. He hurried into the house, brushed his hair and put on his best coat and the shoes with buckles. Lawrence was strolling toward the ravine when he returned and together they hurried to the wharf.

"Lawrence! Tell the captain to have a care for my boxes," Mrs. Washington called after them. "The last time your father ordered goblets, every one was broken on the way."

"I shall see to it," Lawrence promised. "Come, George!"

The children left behind began to fuss.

"I want to ride on the ferry," six-year-old Betty teased.

"I want to go!" Sam planted his feet wide apart and yelled.

Jack was too young to understand but he yelled too.

"Quiet, all of you!" Mrs. Washington commanded. "Better be gone quickly, Lawrence," she called over her shoulder, "or these children will be heard in Fredericksburg."

Laughing, Lawrence and George hurried away. In a few minutes they were aboard the clumsy ferry.

As they pulled away, George looked expectantly at Lawrence.

"So you want to know what this is about?" Lawrence said. "The last time Father came to Hunting Creek, he told me that he was not pleased with Hobby's teaching. A one-room neighborhood school is good for a time. It is convenient and gives you a start. But Father heard that a better school might be opened in Fredericksburg. He wants to know if the rumor is true. We shall not count on it until we see."

The crossing was brief. Before George had time for many questions, the ferry tied up near the sailing ship from England. Lawrence went at once to attend to Mrs. Washington's boxes.

George marveled that Lawrence knew exactly what to say and do as invoices were checked and boxes marked "Fragile" were moved to the ferry under his watchful eye.

"I am lucky to have a brother as wonderful as Lawrence," George thought humbly. "I wonder if I can ever be as smart and as handsome?" It seemed doubtful.

"Now we can leave," Lawrence said in relief. And the two climbed the steep cobblestone road to the town.

George looked around with keen curiosity. He saw the church with the familiar steeple, many houses, a stone jail with iron-barred windows, shops, and people strolling about.

Lawrence inquired of one of these for the residence of the Reverend James Marye and was directed to the parsonage, by the church. The rector was at home, and Lawrence introduced himself and George and accepted the invitation to come inside.

"My father had hoped to call upon you, sir, about the education of my young brother," he explained as they all sat down. "But because of his many duties at his iron works and the task of managing his three plantations, the matter has been postponed. My father has heard that you may open a school. If this is your intention, we would like to enroll my brother."

The Reverend Marye had looked keenly from one Washington to the other while Lawrence was speaking.

"Where did you receive your education?" he asked.

"At Appleby in England," Lawrence told him. "My father lived in England and attended Appleby. Others of our family went to that school and my brother Augustine, Jr., who is near my age, is there. At the proper time my father plans to take George to England, too. Meanwhile, my brother needs good preparation which my father hopes you can give him."

"Have you had any schooling, George?" Marye asked.

"Yes, sir. Master Hobby teaches me reading and writing and sums," George answered respectfully.

Marye turned to his desk and selected a bit of paper and a quill pen.

"Let me see your writing," he said.

George sat down, took the quill, and wrote his name in

his best style. The result was not remarkable. Marye eyed it, frowning.

"Those field schools," he began. Then he paused and rubbed his chin thoughtfully. It was plain he was not favorably impressed with George's instruction. The term "field school" which he used was often applied to a small one-room schoolhouse erected by a group of neighbors. One gave a part of his field, others labor, materials, or tobacco for buying books. The great problem was to find a suitable teacher; the colony of Virginia lacked such men.

"I do better with sums," George ventured to speak up when the silence grew long. "I like arithmetic."

"I hope we are not too late to enter my brother," Lawrence remarked, now a bit anxious at the turn the interview was taking.

"On the contrary, you are too early," Marye answered more cheerfully. "I shall not open my school before autumn, perhaps not until next year. Um-m-m, I wonder if your father has considered the cost of textbooks as well as tuition?"

"My father will not object to any proper charge," Lawrence answered, with due caution about committing his father's purse. "Perhaps you will be good enough to send Father word when your school is about to open?"

"You may count on that," Marye said, now reassured. "Meanwhile, have the boy continue his studies."

The visitors bowed out politely. As they walked down the street, George sighed with relief.

"The Reverend Marye must be a *very* learned man," he said. "He is so very solemn."

"Never mind!" Lawrence answered. "You have to be prepared for Appleby, and Hobby could never do it. Where shall we go now? The ferry can wait."

"I would like to go to the Apothecary's Shop, Lawrence," George said, eagerly. "Our smith has told me about it. The window has two big urns, one red, one green. Candy is for sale," George added hopefully.

Lawrence was willing, and soon they saw the small but enchanting window. Inside, the shop had a luscious fragrance.

"We have some excellent sugar which has just arrived from England," the apothecary told them. He opened a case and took out a shallow wooden bowl in which hunks of a taffylike substance were piled. George's mouth watered as he admired the rich caramel color and watched Lawrence expectantly.

"I shall take two pounds," Lawrence ordered. The apothecary reached for his iron sugar clippers; he used them like tongs to cut off individual portions and place them on the scale.

"Two pounds," he repeated.

"Can you direct us to a baker's shop?" Lawrence asked as he paid for the sugar and handed the sack to George.

"Down the street by the corner there is a good place," the man said.

At the baker's, Lawrence bought caraway comfits. George ate two on the ferry and found them delicious.

"I shall take the rest home for a treat," he decided.

The dining table was set in the wide hall. The stone fire-place was empty this June day, but the hearth was cheerful with bright brasses and an embroidered fire screen. A gold-framed mirror hung on one wall and opposite a handsome floor clock ticked off seconds. Leather-bottomed chairs were set up to a large table covered with a linen tablecloth and set with china and pewter. The children stood by their chairs as their mother entered.

"We saw the ferry coming so we waited dinner," she said. "George has learned to say grace, Lawrence. We are ready, son."

They stood with bowed heads while George recited: "God bless us for what we are about to receive." Then they sat down.

A young serving maid hovered over the children, tying bibs, while an older woman brought food from the kitchen. In Virginia this was often a separate building; the danger of fire was less, and flies, drawn by cooking, were kept from the dining room.

The woman set a large platter before Lawrence, who carved the two roast chickens. Then she brought sliced ham, a bowl of greens cooked with bacon, blackberry jam, butter, hot cornbread, and handleless cups of hot tea. Later she passed wheat bread and a large bowl piled with fruit picked that morning, early plums, cherries and red currants.

As they were finishing the meal, Lawrence winked at George, who promptly produced the comfits and the sugar.

"I shall persuade Father to take *me* to town soon," Betty

announced as she found the last crumb and plunked it into her mouth. George chuckled. They both knew their father had no time for shopping journeys.

The other children drifted out of doors. George sat quietly as Lawrence talked with Mrs. Washington about the school and left messages for his father. Until last winter the Wash-

ingtons had all lived at Hunting Creek farm and Mrs. Washington was interested in the place.

"Perhaps your father will come to Hunting Creek soon," she remarked as Lawrence rose to leave.

"I wish he would bring George with him," Lawrence said. "That is, if you can spare him?" George's face brightened and Mrs. Washington half promised.

Striding along by Lawrence, George went to the horse lot where he mounted Whitefoot to ride as far as the main road.

"I wish you could stay longer, Lawrence," George said.

"And who would do my work at Hunting Creek?" scoffed Lawrence. "Lucky for me the day is long so I can get home before dark. But you will be coming to visit me, George. Don't tease Father. Better be surprised when he mentions a visit. Then you may say that I will teach you farming and care of the stock. He will like that, and you will enjoy it more than school." Laughing, Lawrence touched his horse lightly and was on his way.

George rode back to the barn. The Washingtons had slaves to do the work at Ferry farm, but Mr. Washington had told George that a boy old enough to have his own horse must take care of it. That was no hardship; George liked keeping Whitefoot's stall clean, bedding the pony with fresh straw, and measuring out the feed. Usually he talked as he curried and cared for his pony. But today his thoughts were with Lawrence. The prospect of a visit at Hunting Creek farm was far more interesting than a new school.

Lawrence Goes to War

The promised visit to Hunting Creek farm was delayed by two happenings; a new baby sister was born and, after that, Mr. Washington had furnace trouble at the iron works. George grew very impatient.

"Maybe we will *never* go," he grumbled to Whitefoot as his pony drank at the water trough. "Lawrence was here in June. Now July is nearly over."

But that very day, at dinner, Gus Washington glanced at George as he arose from the table. "Think you would like to ride with me as far as Hunting Creek farm, George?" he asked.

"Oh, Father! Yes!" George cried. "Do we start today?"

His father smiled. "You will not be so eager, time we get halfway there. I ride fast and shall stay but one night."

"George could visit a while," his mother suggested. "Lawrence will look after him, Gus."

"May I, Father?" George asked eagerly.

His father nodded. "If your mother approves. We shall start early tomorrow. Better pack the saddle bags tonight, Mary."

Early the next morning the two set off, George on Whitefoot, who was a good traveler, though small, and Mr. Washington on a sturdy mount that had taken him countless miles between his many properties. For an hour they rode steadily in the cool shade of a forest trail. After a while they splashed through a swift flowing creek and dismounted.

"I like this spring—see, by the moss?" Mr. Washington pointed to a stream of clear water bubbling from the ground by a log. "It will pay us to rest here awhile."

They drank from the spring while they breathed their horses. Then, after watching to see that the animals drank slowly, the riders stretched out by the creek to rest. Gus Washington looked around contentedly; the forest was very beautiful.

"My grandfather was a wise man to buy large acreage on the Northern Neck," he remarked. "He chose good land, too."

George looked at his father with interest. That sentence had two new ideas—a man he knew nothing of and the words "Northern Neck." *"Your* grandfather!" he exclaimed. "That would be my *great* grandfather!"

"Yes," Washington agreed. "John Washington. He was the son of an English rector. He shipped as mate on a sailing vessel, *The Sea Horse,* in 1657." Washington leaned back on his elbow and grinned at George's wide-eyed interest. "It is time you were learning something of your family, son. My grandfather liked Virginia better than England. But he had contracted as mate for the round trip and a Washington keeps his word. A Virginia gentleman got John a legal release from his contract. John married his benefactor's daughter.

"John did well with property his wife inherited. He built a good house near Pope's Creek and called the place by that name. You were born there, son. I like that place; we would be there yet only I have other land and the iron works up this way. That spot was the first Washington home in the colony. You were too young to remember the salt marshes, the ducks and good fishing. Some day I shall take you there.

"That land gave John a start, but he was more than a farmer," Mr. Washington continued. "He made a business of bringing settlers to Virginia; got paid fifty acres for each one. He built a grist mill, fought Indians, was a colonel—your great grandfather was quite a man."

"Was your father like him?" George asked.

"Not a bit. Men differ widely, even men in the same family. My father, Lawrence, inherited most of his father's property—that was the way of the time. He did well enough with it. But he was more interested in public service than in land. He became a justice of the peace, sheriff, and a member of the house of burgesses. That means he was a delegate in the lower branch of the colonial government of Virginia," Washington added when he saw that his words had no meaning to George.

"John and Lawrence and Augustine," George repeated the Washington names. "But I am George."

"Your mother named you for her guardian, who was good to her when her parents died," Washington said as he rose from

They drank from the spring while they breathed their horses. Then George and his father stretched out by the creek to rest.

the bank and had a good stretch. He was a handsome man, six feet and more tall, blond, and very strong. "We had better be on our way, son, if we expect to get to Hunting Creek for dinner." He pulled the horses from the creek, and they mounted.

As they rode, George turned his father's talk over in his mind. At their next pause he had a question ready.

"You said your Grandfather John had land on the 'Northern Neck.' Where is that, Father?"

"All this!" Washington waved his arm widely. "In his day most Virginians lived south of here, around Yorktown and Williamsburg. This section was wilderness. Only a few like John ever thought of it. Even twenty-five years ago when I was a youth, talk was all about England this and England that. People looked across the sea for everything. Country up here was not developed. The Northern Neck I mentioned is the upper part of the land between the Potomac and Rappahannock rivers. You were born here, son; you have always lived in these 'backwoods.'

"Now, each year, more men are thinking about the West. A man hears that out west, beyond the mountains, there are thousands and thousands of acres of fine country. Maybe people will go there and make homes. Grandfather thought they would.

"We have not done badly for ourselves up here, George," he added in a tone that thrilled his son because Washington was talking to him man to man. "I am glad I bought that

Hunting Creek farm and built a house there. I like the location."

"I like it there better than at Ferry farm," George ventured to say. "I like the wide river and ships loading at our wharf."

"Naturally you do," Washington agreed kindly. "The Rappahannock is too narrow up our way for the big ships. But I needed Ferry farm—I bought it because it is near the iron works. And I wanted more land. A man needs a lot of land under cultivation when he grows tobacco, son."

"Were there any Indians around here, Father?" George had wondered about this.

"Not many. Once there was an Indian village across from Hunting Creek; our land was once called Epsewassen. Now most of the Indians have moved west of the Blue Ridge mountains."

Washington rolled over, cupped his two strong hands and drank deeply from the brook. Then they rode many more miles.

When father and son arrived at Hunting Creek farm, they found the stable yard in a turmoil. Two strange horses, flecked with lather, were being unsaddled and groomed. Smoke was pouring from the kitchen chimney; sound of talk came from the west door. Washington tossed his bridle to a slave and hurried into the house. George dismounted and followed.

Inside a group of men were about to dine. Lawrence turned, and his face lighted when he saw his father.

"I am so glad you came today," he said in a relieved tone.

"Word has just come from Williamsburg—there is war!"

"War!" Washington had seen that something was up but this was not expected. "Where?" he asked incredulously.

Looking around the table he saw his friend William Fairfax, owner of a large plantation nearby.

"Tell me, William," he asked, "does Lawrence understand rightly?"

"He does indeed, Gus," Fairfax answered. "These gentlemen have just brought the news." He turned to introduce the visitors, but Washington quickly greeted them. They were men he had met in Williamsburg.

"Spain claims English land to the south—called Georgia," Fairfax went on when greetings were over. "Our king has called for troops from the colonies. These friends tell us that in the towns young men are eager to enlist."

"I should like to go myself," Lawrence said quickly. "Could you spare me, Father?"

Serving maids brought in food at this moment: tempting roast ducks, crisp and brown from the spit; a large blue china platter of sliced ham; a bowl of sallet-greens; baskets of bread and plates of steaming cornbread, fragrant and golden.

"Seat yourselves, gentlemen," Washington invited. "Rest and eat. No doubt the King's business can wait the brief time you need for refreshment." There was a bustle of seating, filling plates and glasses. No one noticed a young boy. George did not expect more than Lawrence's glance of warm welcome.

"Virginia is to send four regiments with young men from

our colony to officer them," one of the Williamsburg men said. "Admiral Vernon and his fleet will attack the Spanish Main."

"Of course you will enlist, Lawrence," Washington finally said in reply to his son's question. But as he listened to war talk Washington wondered how he could manage three farms and the iron works without this capable son.

Dinner took a long time, for the talk was lively. After awhile the cook sent in an elegant Tipsy Squire pudding, a dessert of cake, cream, and nuts she had hastily made.

When he was free, George wandered outdoors to look at the wide, peaceful river. He could not imagine war. He could not even imagine an Indian village over there, beneath the trees. Suddenly he was weary. He went around to the stables where he could talk to the grooms and feel the quiet rhythm of animals being cared for with skill and kindness. Horses were something he knew.

Later the messengers and neighbors went away. Washington called his sons to him, and they sat under the trees, high above the river, and planned what Lawrence should do.

"Go to Williamsburg," Washington said. "Inform yourself and apply for a commission. I can give you a list of men to see for influence." Augustine Washington held only local offices: justice of the peace, sheriff, vestryman of Truro Parish, but he had many friends in high places in the colony.

"And Lawrence, if you hear of a well-recommended man who could help me with the farm, have him ride here at once. I shall need such a one." They talked until George went to bed.

When he wakened in the morning, George found that his father had already left for Ferry farm. Lawrence went to Williamsburg the next day. But there was plenty to interest a boy on the river and in the barns. When his father came to fetch him a few days later, George found life at Master Hobby's school and a home full of small children very dull by contrast.

Months later Reverend Marye opened his school in the front room of the parsonage. Several boys, most of them from Fredericksburg, enrolled along with George. Marye was willing to board a pupil during the week, but Mrs. Washington preferred that George live at home and ferry across each day.

During the spring when George was eight, school was interrupted by several visits to Hunting Creek farm. Lawrence tried to have George do a little reading, but not much was done. He took the boy with him as he rode about inspecting the farm. Lawrence was restless, daily expecting his commission.

A neighbor, William Fairfax, invited the brothers to Belvoir, his beautiful estate nearby. Lawrence liked the company of the daughter, Anne, and her father was amused by George.

"Never did I see such a tall lad as you," he said to George. "Eight years old you say?"

"Eight years last February," George said, being accurate.

"Hands as big as mine." Fairfax held his out. "I'll wager you could trail a fox. I have a dog to train. Come ride with me."

Weeks passed pleasantly and no one mentioned school. It was June when Lawrence's commission was received, but the transport did not come for him until October.

George was at Hunting Creek when a ship flying the royal flag tied up at the wharf. He peered down, entranced, seeing the sailors in bright uniforms, the two fierce cannon, the fluttering flags. Lawrence had been ready for weeks. Now he hurried from the house, friends and servants trailing behind.

"Good-by, George!" he shouted to the lad on the high bank. "Take care of everything for me!"

George tried to answer, but his throat was tight; no word came. Lawrence was hardly aboard when the captain shouted an order and sailors cast off. The ship swung gently into the current. Sails flapped. The helmsman turned the wheel, rudder ropes groaned, and canvas caught the breeze.

"Good-by, Lawrence!" George shouted belatedly. "Good-by!" But Lawrence was too far away to hear. George stood there a long time, watching until the beautiful ship was out of sight around the distant bend.

Many Changes

After months without word from the West Indies a letter that Lawrence had written in Jamaica arrived. George was astonished that Lawrence wrote more about smallpox and yellow fever than about glorious battles. After more months word came that the war had turned to Georgia; the fleet was not needed, and Virginians were coming home.

Lawrence arrived late in 1742 and was received with honor by the colony. Later the governor appointed him military adjutant in recognition of his war service, an office that gave him charge of the militia of Virginia.

The returned warrior found changes at Ferry farm. The baby sister had died. Austin, Lawrence's brother who had expected to study law in England, had come home to help his father. He was learning to manage the farm at Pope's Creek.

"I had George visit me for a time," Austin told Lawrence. "He is good company." Lawrence saw that the two got on well.

But George soon showed his family that no one took Lawrence's place in his affections. Now his hero was more fascinating than ever; he had seen foreign places and could tell tales of ships and battles. Lawrence had served on the flagship and was the friend of a real admiral. George followed his brother around and begged to be allowed to go back with him to Hunting Creek.

"And leave school?" Lawrence exclaimed. "Are you failing?"

"Oh, no, Lawrence!" George was shocked. "But I could learn more with you."

Lawrence grinned understandingly. But George stayed in school.

After gay holidays with six sons and daughter Betty crowding the modest house, the older sons went back to work. At Pope's Creek, Austin was trying to set up a business of raising fine horses, much needed in the colony. Lawrence, at Hunting Creek, planned to erect a few needed buildings and clear more fields for growing tobacco. He had told his father that he hoped to marry Anne Fairfax in the spring. As for Gus Washington, he continued his heavy round of duties at his Accokeek Iron Works, Hunting Creek, Pope's Creek, and Ferry farm.

The iron business had first been successful in America in 1717, with a Maryland furnace owned by an English firm. There Gus Washington learned how to take ore from the ground, smelt it, and ship it to England. Colonists were not allowed to make durable goods; that profitable business was reserved for England.

Washington built furnaces, prepared wood for charcoal from his own forests and built ships for transport. All this required scores of laborers who must be housed and fed. Wagons, tools, and all sorts of supplies were needed, and craftsmen, too; wagonwrights, blacksmiths, millers, sawyers, carpenters, and others. Slaves could be trained to the work under a skilled manager, but this last was a hard job to fill. Gus Washington had to be his own manager much of the time.

As for George, he did so well in school that his father planned an Easter vacation for him—a visit to his cousins in another county. George was there, in the midst of a day of sports, when a messenger arrived from Ferry farm.

"Your father is ill—very ill!" the man cried as he slid from his exhausted horse. "You are to come home at once."

George dashed for Whitefoot. The messenger was loaned a fresh mount and the two galloped home. George arrived in time to see his strong father stretched flat on his bed, too ill to know his son or to speak. Mrs. Washington let him stand there a few minutes, then she motioned him away.

Soon Lawrence came into the hall. "Father is dead."

"Dead!" George exclaimed incredulously. His strong handsome father, the man who had more energy than any person George had ever known—dead? But it was true. This sad loss came a few weeks after George's eleventh birthday.

During those next sad days George thought often of the ride with his father nearly four years before. He was glad to have had that trip and their talk to remember.

After Augustine Washington had been buried in the family burying ground a mile from Pope's Creek, his will was read. George's father had thought of the future of all his children.

Lawrence, the oldest son, was to have the largest plantation, Hunting Creek farm. That was still the custom in the
colony. Austin inherited Pope's Creek farm. George was to
have Ferry farm when he was twenty-one and also some other
land. Sam and Jack and Charles were each given tracts of
several hundred acres and Betty's inheritance was in money.
The forty-nine slaves were divided among the heirs, and each
child and the mother were given shares in the iron company.
Mrs. Washington was to hold and manage her children's property until they became of age.

When this legal business was finally settled, Lawrence and
Austin went back to their homes, and life at Ferry farm settled
down. George missed Lawrence more than ever because now
he had no father.

In July of that year, 1743, Lawrence married Anne Fairfax
and the family reassembled for the wedding. The event, so
soon after Mr. Washington's death, was not as festive as it might
have been, but George thought it very grand. The social life
of Virginia was the most elegant of all the colonies.

This marriage brought many changes in George's life.
Lawrence's bride invited him for a long visit; she told him to
call her Nancy, as Lawrence did. George's mother was willing
to have George stay at Hunting Creek now that Lawrence had
a bride of distinction.

Nancy's father, Colonel William Fairfax, continued his
liking for George. Fairfax was one of the richest and most distinguished men in Virginia; he was a burgess, then a member

of the higher body, the Council, and a year after the wedding was made President of the Council. Next to the governor's palace, his home, Belvoir, was the meeting place of the greatest men in the colony.

George was now eleven and a half and naturally quick to observe people and manners. This association with the Fairfax family had taught him fine manners and habits of graciousness; in a measure, it took the place of the training his father had intended him to have in England.

Lawrence and Nancy lived in the story-and-a-half house that was probably built by Gus Washington before he moved there in the seventeen-thirties. It had a center hall and four rooms downstairs and rooms with dormer windows above. They added furniture and hangings, and Nancy had handsome silver and other choice things. George thought the place very elegant, though, of course, it was not large and handsome like Belvoir.

When the pretty things were all in place Nancy told George they were giving the place a new name.

"This is no longer Hunting Creek farm, George," she said. "We call it Mount Vernon; Mount for the high bank above the river, Vernon for Lawrence's good friend the admiral."

"Mount Vernon." George repeated the words, testing the sound. "That is a good name, Nancy. I like it."

A few days later the Lawrence Washingtons gave a dinner party as a housewarming. The slaves worked early and late with the preparations. They polished silver, washed and ironed

linens, and washed the china and every window in the house.

George wondered if a boy going on twelve would be allowed at the table. Nancy soon relieved his mind about that.

"Lawrence thinks this is a good chance for you to learn about grown-up affairs," she said. "Wear that new suit Lawrence ordered from London. Better try it on today, George, and let Lawrence see if it needs any changes. And, George, will you tell Chloe that I shall be out to inspect every duck myself when she has finished cleaning them? Everything is to be perfect at my first party!"

She bustled about happily, keys clicking at her belt like an experienced housewife. George did the errand and then ran upstairs to try on the suit. It had come only that morning.

The guests were very fashionable. The dinner was delicious, George thought, though he was so excited he could not eat as much as usual—well, not quite as much. When the ladies retired to the drawing room to talk of fashions and household matters, Colonel Fairfax motioned for George to sit by him. The men were talking, at the moment, about war.

"You must feel a satisfaction, Lawrence," a guest across the table remarked, "to know that you could serve the king when he needed you." Lawrence nodded and bowed modestly.

"His majesty needs service in peacetime, too," a man in a green satin coat said. The others looked at him.

"I am thinking of the land west of the mountains," he explained. "Your relative, Lord Fairfax, owns vast acreage.

I believe you manage it for him, Fairfax?"

"If you can call it managing," Colonel Fairfax waved his hand casually. "Actually wilderness land has little value. King Charles the Second would not have given it away, years ago, if he had thought well of it."

"You speak of the Fairfax Proprietary, I take it?" a guest in a bright-blue coat and stylish periwig inquired.

"Yes." Fairfax smiled. "An elegant name for a wild, unsurveyed stretch of country. I had a letter from Lord Fairfax the other day—he asks whether there is a demand by settlers for his land. I do not know what to tell him."

"No demand at all, I'd say," some one spoke up. "Not with Indians only a short journey away. Now if the Indians could be persuaded to move west of the Allegheny Range, a lively trade in land might open up."

"At great profit to us all," Fairfax laughed and raised his glass. The talk went on until the guests' carriages arrived.

That was only the first of many dinner parties at Mount Vernon. How much of the talk—business, military, and political—a boy of twelve could understand, George himself could hardly have told. But he was a thoughtful lad. He turned men's words over in his mind and began growing up.

Occasionally George rode with Lawrence to see Austin at Pope's Creek. This brother urged George to live with him.

"You like to work with horses, George," he said. "And there are boys your own age nearby—the Lee family, and others." But though George did go for one or two visits, he was always glad to return to Mount Vernon. He loved that place.

When he stayed at Ferry farm he found that life very different from either brother's. There, small children, school, and daily tasks under his mother's supervision kept him busy.

Mrs. Washington had considerable help, both slaves and indentured servants. Still, the mother of five children and manager of a farm had a great deal to do. She must guard the children from daily hazards: poison ivy on the river slope, measles, warts, croup (the terror of those days), and chicken pox. She was also the doctor, and she made her own medicines from herbs grown in her garden or searched out in the forest.

The blacksmith was the dentist, though of course the mother pulled "baby teeth." She tied a string from tooth to doorknob and held the child while some one slammed the door —and pulled the tooth. The blacksmith was called in when a "second tooth" ached. Mother held the patient flat on the table while the smith, with a dramatic flourish of black pincers

and sheer strength, yanked out the tooth—and often some bone along with it.

The children all rode horses, too. So the mother must be ready to tie red meat over bruises or set broken bones. It was a busy life, full of surprises.

At school, George studied the classics, writing, algebra, and geometry. Reverend Marye was most particular about writing. He had George copy one hundred and ten rules from an old English volume called *The Rules of Conduct.*

"Write each rule over and over until you have it perfect," the master ordered. "I shall accept no carelessly made letters."

So George wrote in his copybook:

"Mock not, nor jest at anything of importance; break no jests that are sharp biting, and if you deliver anything witty or pleasant, abstain from laughing at it yourself.

"When you see a crime punished, you may be inwardly pleased; but always show pity to the suffering offender.

"Labor to keep alive in your breast that little spark of celestial fire called conscience."

This chore of copying over and over to satisfy his teacher taught George the easy, flowing handwriting that was to be so important to him later.

One Saturday his mother set him at the tedious task of cleaning the storehouse. This was a small building, near the kitchen, where countless articles were put when not in daily use. He moved boxes and bundles. He scrubbed and sorted under her keen eye until someone called her away. While alone,

George rummaged in a dark corner. There he found an odd thing made up of iron rods and chains. As his mother returned she heard the sounds he made examining the thing.

"Now what have you there?" she demanded.

"I don't know, Mother," George said. "Do you?"

When she saw what he was holding, she laughed. "Of course I know! That's your father's surveying chain; did you never see it before? His compass is in the desk. Your father always surveyed property he bought to make sure of the boundaries."

"Father knew everything, didn't he?" George said quietly.

Something in the lad's tone caught his mother's attention. She put her hand on his shoulder in a rare gesture of affection.

"Not everything, son," she answered kindly. "But he was a fine man. He had more knowledge than most men in the colony. But a chain is no good to us now. Take it to the smith; he can use the metal." Mary Washington was her practical self again.

"May I keep it because it was Father's?" George asked.

"Oh, yes, if you like. After you have scrubbed the floor, put it in the corner, there. It does not take much room."

She bustled away, the keys at her belt jingling. "He will soon forget," she thought. "Then the smith can have it."

George finished the scrubbing and put the brush and bucket away. As he laid the long chain in the corner he made a promise to himself.

"Monday I shall begin to learn surveying."

A Young Surveyor

All the next day George was restless and uneasy. He had never asked a favor of the Reverend Marye. How should he word his request to learn surveying?

While he curried Whitefoot, George muttered to himself, saying over sentences and tactful approaches. None seemed good. Marye was a stern man, aloof from his pupils. George went to bed Sunday still puzzled as to what he should say.

Monday morning, George was waiting at the dock when the ferryman came. When they crossed the river, he hurried up the hill to school. Marye was at his desk, but the other pupils had not yet arrived. George walked to the desk and spoke quickly, but respectfully.

"Good morning, sir. Will you please teach me to be a surveyor?"

Marye stared at him, astonished. George shifted his weight from his left to his right foot and locked his hands behind him. He never quite knew what to do with hands when Marye got that pained expression on his stern face.

"I have found my father's surveying tools," George explained, "and I would like to learn to use them."

Marye frowned at the urgency in George's tone.

"You have a strange notion about your rate of progress," he complained. "A surveyor needs trigonometry and logarithms which you have not yet studied. When I consider that you are ready, we may, perhaps, speak of this again. Now get to the lesson of today."

George turned and walked to his bench. His hands trembled with rage, and his blood was hot. Trigonometry? Logarithms? If he needed those subjects, why didn't Marye teach them?

"I am top boy in arithmetic," George thought rebelliously. "Yet he talks to me as though I were young Sam." He took a quill and pulled out his knife to whittle a point. But his eyes were blurred with rage. The quill was soon a heap of scraps.

James, his seatmate, watched him with amusement. "Wish I'd got here earlier," he thought. "The master's got old George in a rage this time. Wonder what's up?"

George picked up a second quill, sharpened it and began to write. But his hand raced angrily over the paper. The day was half gone before he could put his mind on his work.

Later, at home, George went to the storeroom and handled the surveyor's chain. It was long and heavy; the links rattled mysteriously in the dim light.

"Father would have taught me," George assured himself. "He would like me to be a surveyor. Marye spoke as though there was much to learn. I must talk with Lawrence."

The first chance to go to Mount Vernon came some weeks

after George's fourteenth birthday. Then Mrs. Washington sent him with a message to Lawrence. It was a Saturday and he arrived in time for dinner. As usual there were guests. But after the meal, Lawrence drew George into his study; he saw that the youth had some special matter on his mind.

"I want to ask you about school—and surveying, Lawrence," George began when they were alone.

"Surveying?" Lawrence said. "Isn't that a new idea?"

"I found Father's chain when Mother and I cleaned the storeroom," George went on. "I asked the master to teach me but he put me off. School is very tiresome, Lawrence. Two of the boys have left for England. James quit this week to help on his father's plantation. New boys are so *young*. I am the tallest and oldest in the room. I want to learn what I need for a *man's* work."

Lawrence stroked his long chin thoughtfully.

"Father meant you to go to England, too. But your mother is not willing for you to be away so long. You would need three or four years—I had to admit that."

George was silent. Perhaps Lawrence had some plan for him.

"I have been wondering about a profession for you. Ferry farm will be yours; but the soil is light. It will not produce a good living by itself. Would you like to go to sea?"

"To sea!" George's jaw dropped in astonishment. "Oh, Lawrence, that would be wonderful!" His eyes glowed, and

George picked up a second quill, sharpened it, and began to write. But his hand raced angrily over the paper.

visions of wide sails and a deck where he was master floated before him. "I would like that vastly better than surveying. How do I begin?"

"Oh, you might get an appointment in the King's navy. Our family has influence, and Colonel Fairfax would help you. Or you might get on a merchant ship out of Yorktown."

"But if Mother will not let me go to England, will she let me join the navy?" George asked in sudden dismay.

"Well, that is a point," Lawrence admitted. "At least we can ask her. I shall ride back with you tomorrow."

The next day, when Lawrence tactfully made his suggestion Mrs. Washington settled the matter at once.

"George is not to go to sea," she said firmly. "Remember, he is my son, not yours, Lawrence Washington."

For a time, George was bitterly disappointed. But with the coming of spring and summer, he began to forget. He continued at school, occasionally visiting Mount Vernon.

In September, Lawrence and Colonel Fairfax stopped at Ferry farm for a brief call.

"We are on our way to see about some land beyond Fredericksburg. I took the opportunity to see that you are all well," Lawrence told Mrs. Washington.

"No, we cannot stay, thank you," Colonel Fairfax replied to her invitation to dinner. "We have to pick up George Byrne and his helpers in town." They chatted briefly and left.

George hung over the fence, watching them down the lane.

"*I* could have helped them," he grumbled. As the riders

turned into the main road he recalled the name "George Byrne."

"He is a surveyor. Maybe *he* could teach me!" Suddenly George felt energetic and amiable. Young Sam was cleaning the water trough in the horse lot. "Want help, Sam?"

Sam stared—and handed over a scrub brush. The boys got the trough clean. Then they watched while the stableman connected up a wooden pipe and filled the trough with fresh spring water.

The next day, George made inquiries at the town wharf.

"George Byrne?" one of the idlers answered. "Sure I know him. Best surveyor around here. He's out on a job now."

George waited several days. Then he went to Byrne's house and pounded on the knocker. A friendly looking man in his middle thirties opened the door.

"I am looking for Mr. George Byrne," George said.

"You've found him." Byrne opened the door wide and motioned for George to enter. The room was a kind of office; surveying tools were scattered over the floor and a long table was littered with maps, papers, inkpots, and quills.

"I am George Washington from Ferry farm, across the river. Perhaps you knew my father, Augustine Washington," George said.

"That I did," Byrne agreed. "I've helped him on many a survey—but that was some time ago."

"Yes, sir," George replied. "And now I want to be a surveyor myself. Would you teach me?"

"What do you want to be a surveyor for?" Byrne asked curiously. "You have a farm to manage."

"My mother will manage the land for some years yet," George explained, flushing. "Since I found my father's surveying chain, I have the urge to learn that profession. I can figure and keep accounts," he added with a glance at the littered table. "And I could go with you and carry the rod and chain."

"Um-m-m." Byrne was thoughtful. George had seen a gleam in his eye when figures were mentioned, so he enlarged that point.

"I could make a map like this, sir, if you would let me."

"Surveying is not all gentlemen's work, sitting at a table," Byrne said quickly, "though that is important—and I hate it. You'd have hours of tramping in the mud, climbing mountains, wading creeks—you'd hardly care for all that." He eyed George curiously.

"I like the outdoors, sir," George said. "All you say makes me want to learn the more."

"Well, then," Byrne rose, his mind made up, "come tomorrow. I'll leave here at eight. Wear your topboots, son, you'll need 'em."

"Shall I bring my chain, sir?" George asked hopefully.

"Not tomorrow. You'll lug mine."

They were gone four days. Byrne found his helper useful. He told George to come on Tuesday of the next week. New settlers were arriving west of town and wanted boundary lines surveyed before they built cabins. Fortunately this was spring vacation when George often went visiting, so his mother did not object.

During that summer George took several trips with Byrne. Occasionally he served as rodman for other Fredericksburg surveyors. He learned to measure the boundaries of a piece of land, to stake corners or note a certain tree as a marker. He learned to set the measurements on a map and to show rivers and creeks. His drawing was neat and the lettering clear; the owner was sure to be satisfied. He also got a book of logarithms and studied it.

On a visit to Mount Vernon, George surveyed Lawrence's turnip field and some hilly land nearby. Lawrence was astonished and very pleased at the neat maps.

One day Byrne handed George two pounds in pay—real money, not tobacco, which was more often used as money in the colony.

"Mine?" he exclaimed, amazed.

Byrne grinned. "You're doing a man's job—no reason why you shouldn't be paid for it."

The future seemed dazzling. George liked his work, and he liked having his own money. He started an account book, saved his earnings, and felt manly and affluent. He doubted that he would go back to Marye's school the next year.

In the late autumn of 1747 when George was nearing sixteen, Lord Thomas Fairfax came to Belvoir for a long visit. He was the owner, George remembered, of the great tract of land which men called the Fairfax Proprietary—six million or more acres in the Northern Neck. Peter Jefferson (father of four-year-old Thomas) and Joseph Fry had risked great danger trying to survey this land between the Potomac and the Rappahannock rivers. But the survey was never completed.

Lord Fairfax had come from England to see about this land. He was a middle-aged man with many oddities of dress and manner. George enjoyed his tales of England; if his father had lived he would be seeing those interesting places himself.

But his lordship was not the only attraction at Belvoir. Nancy's young sister Sarah had suddenly blossomed into a pretty young lady, and a friendship with Nancy's older brother, George William Fairfax, was developing. George Washington had had little contact with young people except at Belvoir and he enjoyed them. As it turned out, those friendships brought him his first important business opportunity.

On a late winter day, the Lawrence Washingtons and George rode over to Belvoir to call. They found Lord Fairfax pacing the floor excitedly. He held an open letter in his hand and shook its pages as he talked.

"Squatters moving onto my land!" he exclaimed angrily. "They claim the land belongs to anyone who is there to use it!" His lordship strode the length of the room nervously.

"Lord Fairfax has a letter by the post from Philadelphia," Sarah explained to George. "It says that many settlers are moving into his Proprietary. One gathers that he doesn't like it." Sarah smiled at George, amused at her relative's anger.

"You cannot do anything until you have a full survey,"
Colonel Fairfax said patiently. "I have told you that, sir."

"Then get a survey now," his lordship snapped. "You have
written to—what is that man's name?"

"James Genn, surveyor for Prince William County," the
colonel said. "The best man in the Northern Neck."

"All right. If he is that good he will not wait around for
warm weather. Get him off now. I have to know my rights."
Lord Fairfax subsided into a big chair as Sarah and her father
gave their attention to their visitors.

George followed Sarah to the spinet. As they talked, her
fingers made a soft melody of chords.

Presently George noticed Colonel Fairfax, addressing Lawrence.

"While Genn is there, he could survey that land you and
I bought. We might make a nice profit if we had plots ready
to sell."

"That is good sense," Lawrence agreed.

"My son wants to go with Genn," Fairfax continued,
"though he would be no help. Why not have your brother go
too? I hear he is doing well with his surveying. How about
it, George?"

"Sir!" George was taken aback to have a question called
across the room. Colonel Fairfax grinned and explained.

George's eyes gleamed. "I would like it very much, sir,"
he answered fervently.

"But William," Lawrence protested, "George is barely sixteen! Genn's trip is important. He may not care to have a boy along."

"Boy!" Fairfax chuckled. "You talk like an older brother! Look at George—he's grown-up! Likely the tallest in the party. Rides better than most. I wager he knows more about land than any helper Genn will have along."

George flushed and Lawrence said, "Well then. . . ."

So the surveying party was planned. George put extra boots and clothing in his saddle bags. Then he put in a parchment-covered blank book. That was to be his diary of the journey.

George Washington and George William Fairfax left Belvoir on the second Friday in March. They rode forty miles through pouring rain to Neville's Ordinary, an inn where they stayed the first night. The next day they rode on and met Genn and his supply train. Genn had helpers for carrying two tents, supplies of salt meat and cornmeal, and his tools.

They crossed the Blue Ridge mountains at Ashby's Gap and the first sight of the Shenandoah Valley thrilled George. They traveled on through the little village of Winchester to Thomas Cresap's place, a center for fur traders near the place where the South Branch pours into the Potomac.

George wanted to study the stockade and storehouse carefully but he was interrupted by the arrival of a party of thirty Indians. They talked loudly to Cresap and seemed to be complaining.

"Is anything wrong?" George asked Cresap.

"They've been on the warpath," Cresap replied, "and they're annoyed because they caught no white settlers. They got only one white scalp."

George had a sudden queasy feeling in the pit of his stomach. Genn's party, including himself, were white men!

Cresap noticed his face and roared with laughter. "We don't count. I'm a trader, and you're my friend. Indians never scalp a man who is useful to them—only settlers who take the land."

The answer was a relief, but George continued to eye the visitors with fascination mixed with horror. They were quite unlike any Indians he had seen, so he wrote of them in his diary:

". . . we had a War Daunce there manner of Dauncing is . . . They clear a Large Circle and make a Great Fire in y. middle then seats themselves around it y. Speaker makes a grand speech telling them in what Manner they are to Daunce after he had finished y. best Dauncer jumps up as one awaked out of a sleep and runs and jumps about y. Ring in a most comical Manner he is followed by y. Rest . . ." George admired the gourds they rattled and their drum, made of deerskin stretched over a container of water.

He wrote all this and more by firelight, with his diary upon his knee, and with original ideas about spelling. Indeed, words were not too well spelled in school until after Samuel Johnson published his dictionary five years later.

From Cresap's, Genn took his party northwest as far as

Wills Creek on the North Branch. George's work was to take field notes of boundaries, and his knowledge of trees was of great service. Often an old deed would give as a boundary "large hickory and a red oak" or "two redbuds and a black walnut." George could recognize trees at a distance and soon he was acting as second man on the surveying team.

They met few people until early in April when they came across a few Germans from Pennsylvania, who followed Genn's party for some hours. George tried to talk with some and was astonished that he could not understand their replies.

"They're as stupid as Indians," he complained to Genn.

The surveyor laughed. "They're not stupid. They speak German. They cannot understand you, either." This was George's first experience with a foreign language.

On "Fryday" the eighth of April he wrote: ". . . we Camped this Night in ye Woods near a Wild Meadow where was a Large Stack of Hay after we Pitched our Tent and made a very Large Fire we pull'd out our Knapsack . . . every (one) was his own Cook our Spits was Forked Sticks our Plates was a large Chip as for Dishes we had none". This was a night after they had shot wild turkeys.

George was sorry when the five weeks' journey ended. Beds at Mount Vernon were comfortable; food was the best. But there was a thrill about wilderness travel that he had never known on a plantation. He wondered how and when he could take such a journey again.

New Visions

After that journey with Genn, George seemed to be accepted almost as an adult among the neighbors around Mount Vernon. Lawrence and the Fairfaxes read and discussed his diary. Men asked his opinion on land and found that he had noticed more about soil and drainage than had Genn.

Perhaps part of the changed attitude came from George's different feeling about himself. The trip had opened up a new world to this sixteen-year-old, a world without the conforts he had taken for granted. He found that he could roll up in a blanket, sleep on the ground, and go on riding all the next day. He felt an assurance about his surveying, too, now that Genn approved his work. The labor of teaching himself trigonometry and draftsmanship had paid. Now when men talked about land beyond the Blue Ridge, he could join in.

"I should like to own land in the Shenandoah Valley," Lawrence remarked at dinner one day.

"Is it not too far away?" young Fairfax objected. "How would you ship your crop?"

"I should not worry about shipping, now," George Washington spoke confidently. "Of course, shipping is easy, here by the river. But tobacco wears the soil. What will you do when farms along the rivers are exhausted?"

"The fur trade may be our most profitable business," Lawrence suggested. "There is no future in iron so long as England forbids our making durable goods. We shall have to look to fur—and land—for making money."

"As settlers come in they have their own notions about different crops," George added. "They give us a chance to see what the soil will do with hemp, corn, and grains."

"What's land sell for, George?" Colonel Fairfax asked.

"Oh, the price varies." George looked thoughtful. "You can get a hundred acres for from five to seven pounds, I'd say." Talk turned into a discussion of soil and crops.

After the guests left, Lawrence put his hand on George's shoulder affectionately.

"You know, George," he said, "I've regretted that you were not educated in England. But I begin to see that what you have learned here may be more useful than what other youths are learning abroad. Virginia has to find a future here. I look to you to have a part in it."

George flushed. Praise from his hero was sweet.

As time passed, George began to feel that Mount Vernon was his home, not just a place to visit. He never formally left Ferry farm; he came and went there, as his work required. But Nancy and Lawrence made him very welcome and gradually their home became his.

On a bright October day in that year, 1748, George rode

home after a long trip westward. As he came near the mansion, things seemed very quiet. Then he recalled that Lawrence would be in Williamsburg, attending the meeting of the burgesses. Nancy, of course, would be occupied with the new baby, Mildred. A slave took his horse, and George entered the house.

"Oh, *George!* I'm so glad you are here!" Nancy was near the foot of the stairs. She ran lightly toward him and threw her arms around him in an unusual display of emotion.

"I'm glad to be home myself," George admitted, pleased with the welcome. "Did Lawrence get off all right?"

"Get off!" Nancy exclaimed. "He's sick in bed and coughing his poor head off every time he tries to speak. He'll be glad to see you. He frets so about letters and work."

George pulled off his heavy boots and put on lighter shoes. "How's the baby?" he asked.

"I'm worried about her, too, George," Nancy admitted and a sadness came into her face. George was shocked. He knew that Nancy and Lawrence wanted a big family. He had felt their grief when two baby daughters had been born—and died.

"Little Mildred is not as strong as we would wish, George," Nancy said. "The doctor was here yesterday to see both patients. He says Lawrence has 'lung consumption' and must be very careful. With you here to attend to business for him, Lawrence may stop worrying. The doctor says that would help him."

George stayed a fortnight. He wrote letters, did farm inspections, and got accounts in order. Lawrence improved daily. When George left on his next surveying trip his brother was up and around and the household was in better spirits.

When he returned in December, George found the neighborhood astir with social plans. The Fairfaxes had gone south for George William's marriage to Sally Cary. The Carys had a plantation on the James River. Sally was said to be a beauty.

"The Fairfaxes are giving a Christmas ball for the bride and groom," Nancy told George. "They have invited scores of guests. We are putting up several—you'll not mind taking a little room, George? Luckily your suit has come from England. Everyone is agog about what to wear."

Clothes had only recently begun to interest young George. When he went to his room now, he took out a list of things he had written down as necessary for packing when he was invited for a visit.

"Razor, nine shirts, a cloth waistcoat," he read. "Six linen waistcoats, four neck cloths, six bands (to wear under the neckcloth) and seven caps." He opened the wardrobe and inspected his blue satin coat and white breeches. Would these be all right for a great ball? It would be the most elegant party he had ever attended. He must ask Nancy about his clothes.

For a week George fretted about his ruffles, his hair, the fit of the new coat, and the ironing of his lace jabot. Nancy was amused and then exasperated. But when they drove off the day of the ball George looked very handsome.

After the long sumptuous dinner, the rooms were cleared for dancing. George watched the first two or three numbers while his eyes followed the beautiful bride. Never had he seen such a fascinating woman! In the next interval between dances he went to her and bowed low, his right hand over his heart.

"May I have the pleasure of the next dance, ma'am?"

"You're George Washington, my husband's friend," the bride answered gaily. "See how well I notice? And you are to call me Sally and stop being so formal." She took his arm and they strolled to their places on the floor. George was enchanted.

The harpist twanged a chord, signalling that the dance was to begin. The fiddler began the minuet, and dancers moved to and fro in a graceful pattern.

"You dance well, George," Sally remarked after they had done a few measures. "I hardly expected to find a skilled partner so far from Williamsburg."

"Thank you," George said. "I had lessons from a music master. I paid him three shillings ninepence. I'm glad you think he earned his money."

Perhaps it was at this Christmas ball that George began to notice the words "Ohio Company" cropping up in men's talk. By spring he knew that a struggle for the profits of the fur trade was going on. Lawrence and the Fairfaxes were in the Ohio Company—and other companies were forming. George listened thoughtfully to his brother's plans.

"We need a fort near the Ohio River," Lawrence said, "and a trading post. We must have a seaport on the Potomac. Then we can get Indian supplies going up and furs coming down. All this will make settlers feel safe and we can sell land. We can't lose."

"Will the Indians work with you?" George asked.

"Cresap says they will. He has joined the company."

But while this was interesting, none of it seemed to concern George until, some time later, he heard that the Virginia Assembly had given permission for that seaport. The location chosen was nine miles from Mount Vernon at the point where Great Hunting Creek flows into the Potomac.

Years before, a huge tobacco warehouse had been built on the point. Quite a little village grew up around it, called Belle Haven. Now the place was to be a town, Alexandria. Streets would be laid out and lots sold; there would be work for a surveyor. Between two jobs, George rode home to talk with Lawrence about the new town.

When he arrived at Mount Vernon he found the driveway crowded with riders and such a yapping of dogs that voices could hardly be heard.

"You're just in time to join us," George William Fairfax called. "Father bought two new dogs and we're trying them out on a fox."

George hesitated, and Lawrence rode near.

"I came in to talk with you about surveying in Alexandria, Lawrence. Do you know who has the job there?"

"Yes, John West Jr. is the official surveyor," Lawrence said. "I hear he is hiring helpers. Tell him I sent you," he added as George wheeled his restless horse.

"You shouldn't work so hard, George," Colonel Fairfax called as he cantered by. "I hear there's to be a new surveyor appointed in Culpepper County—you'll be after that next!"

The fox hunters turned left and George took the road toward the new town up river. There he found West, who promptly engaged George as assistant surveyor. George was to furnish his own helper and tools as usual.

There was work for some weeks during which time George found out about the job in Culpepper county.

"The President and Masters of the College of William and Mary have control of that job," West told him. "You'd have to go to Williamsburg and take an examination."

"Think I could pass it?" George asked. The idea startled him. He had never taken such an examination.

"Of course you could!" West laughed.

When work at Alexandria slackened, George rode south. He passed the examination and got the position. He took the oath of office on July 2, 1749 when he was a few months past seventeen years old. This was his first public office. He felt a thrill of pride as he rode home to tell Lawrence.

His elation was short-lived. When he got to Mount Vernon he found Lawrence ill again. It had been decided that the sick man should take a voyage to England.

"The doctor says the voyage will be good for him," Nancy told George. "He will consult London physicians."

"And I shall do some business for the Ohio Company," Lawrence said. "You will be here often, George? And look after Nancy?"

George promised and a few days later, Lawrence sailed.

Surveying in Culpepper county opened up slowly. George had time to work in Alexandria, and keep track of things at Mount Vernon, nearby. Lawrence returned in the late autumn, rested but otherwise no better. But he bravely insisted he could manage, and George set off to do some surveying for Lord Fairfax. His lordship had wearied of the gaiety at Belvoir and had built a house near the village of Winchester, on his estates. He called the place Greenway Court. George was invited to live there any time.

Now that George was a qualified surveyor, he could do legal surveys anywhere in the colony. He hired a helper whom he usually paid two shillings sixpence a day. Other expenses were upkeep of two horses, paper, and such items. An average small survey paid three pounds and took one or two days; the work was very profitable. George was busy every day that weather allowed him to work.

Early in the spring, George and Tim, his helper, were riding south in the Valley. The sun was emerging from heavy rain clouds. Their greatcoats were cold and wet, when George noticed smoke drifting over the treetops.

"We could do with a roof and a fire tonight," he said.

"New folks here, maybe?" Tim's tone was hopeful. "Nobody was here when we came through before."

They crossed a creek and soon came upon a clearing and a tiny cabin. A man lounging at the door hurried toward them.

"Caint you stop the night with us, strangers?" he said. "Betsy'n me's that lonesome. If you kin stan' sleeping on the floor like us, we'll share. And you've a welcome."

Tim was already off his tired horse. As George dismounted Betsy appeared at the door, a baby in her arms and a child peeping from behind her skirts.

"Is they goin' t'stay, John?" she asked eagerly. "I got venison in the pot—there's a-plenty, too. And there's dry wood enough inside fer a long fire."

The cabin was tiny but snug, and the dirt floor was dry. George took off his greatcoat and hung it from two pegs on the wall. Tim put his on the other side of the room. While Betsy hurriedly made corn pone, John talked eagerly, as though he had had no visitors for a long time.

"We come from the coast in late fall," he said. "I got oxen, and a horse—of a sort. Betsy's had luck with goose eggs; she has a nice flock and soon we'll have a feather bed. You see I got my cabin up and two fields cleared. I plan to put in hemp and rye."

Betsy stirred the stew and looked pleased at the attention George gave to her husband's story. The toasting corn pone was fragrant.

John was saying, "I got a patent (a deed) to a hundred acres," when his wife interrupted.

"They must be hungry, Husband. Stew's ready. Pull up and set." She ladled meat and gravy into wooden bowls, and they ate at a rough table. After more talk, they rolled up in bearskins and slept on the floor. The baby and little boy slept, feet together, in a cradle brought over the mountains.

Wilderness living made the comforts of Mount Vernon very welcome and George looked forward, each time, to a gay whirl on his return. Sarah Fairfax had married John Carlyle and lived in Alexandria, but Sally's pretty sister Mary had come for a visit.

All that season of 1750 George worked steadily. One month he earned one hundred and forty pounds. In very bad weather, of course, he could do nothing. In the fall of that year when he was eighteen and a half, he bought three carefully considered pieces of land. The first was a tract of 453 acres. Later, that same month of October, he bought 550 acres from Lord Fairfax. These lands were in the Shenandoah Valley. The next month he bought the third tract—456 acres near Vestal Gap on a creek not far from the upper Potomac. This was much the best land of the three, and for it he paid forty-five down and seventy-seven pounds a few months later.

This was wilderness land and produced no income, but the purchase money was earned by his own hard work. George felt a thrill of pride. Lawrence would be pleased.

But alas, Lawrence was far from well, and the new baby Sarah was far from strong. Little Mildred had died some months before and Nancy's eyes were sad when she saw that this fourth baby was frail, too. Lawrence was an even greater worry. He did not improve even after warm weather came.

"What does the doctor say?" George asked on one of his brief visits.

"He says Lawrence should be in a warm climate this winter," Nancy answered.

"I might go to Barbados," Lawrence remarked thoughtfully. "Gedney Clarke lives there—remember him, Nancy? A connection of the Fairfaxes? He could make living arrangements for me."

"Oh, I wish I could go with you, Lawrence," Nancy cried. "But I dare not take or leave the baby!"

"I shall go with you, Lawrence," George decided quickly.

"No! You are doing so well here," Lawrence protested. "No other nineteen-year-old in the colony has done as much as you have."

But Nancy said, "Thank you, George. Now I feel happier."

A letter was sent to Mr. Clarke and in September of 1751 Lawrence and George set sail from Mount Vernon.

The voyage of five weeks fascinated George. In his method-
ical way he studied sails, charted the ship's course, and found
that navigator's lines were much like those he laid out in surveying. He kept a record of ships they passed and of the
weather.

When the brothers landed they found that Mr. Clarke
had got rooms for them and had engaged a doctor. The out-
look was encouraging until suddenly, George, the healthy one,
was taken very ill. On the third morning, when great red spots
appeared, even George knew that he had smallpox. Most people got this disease, sooner or later, before vaccination was discovered, but it was a calamity to a proud young man. The
angry spots became horrid sores, and George knew that when
they dried, after frightful itching, they would leave small pits
in his skin, which he would carry all his life.

When he was able to write he recorded in his diary: "Was
strongly attacked with the small Pox: sent for Dr. Lanahan
whose attendance was very constant till my recovery, and going
out was not till thursday the 12th of December." He gave
more space to the growing of sugar cane, to pineapples, to the
island's defenses and its bad management of money than to
himself.

Lawrence was about the same, neither better or worse, and
he grew very lonesome for Nancy. He hated the weather,
which was always hot. He worried about George.

"I want you to go home, George," he announced one
morning. "Nancy will be worrying; we do not know whether

she has received our letters. If you were at home, you could attend to your business and mine."

"But, Lawrence!" George exclaimed, amazed.

"I know I am no better," Lawrence interrupted. "Perhaps I should go to Bermuda. Nancy might come there in the spring—or you could join me again."

"I should stay with you, Lawrence," George protested. "Anyway, there is no ship."

"You are wrong!" Lawrence chuckled. It was not often that he could catch his brother in an error. "The good ship *Industry* is loading now for Virginia—Clarke just told me. You must go home on her tomorrow."

So George sailed on the twenty-second of December. He hated to leave Lawrence. The weather was frightful, and his face was blotched and red with slow-healing smallpox scars. That voyage home was one of the worst times he had ever known.

Major Washington

George arrived in Yorktown in late January of 1752. He rode the fifteen miles to Williamsburg on a hired horse to deliver a letter Lawrence had sent to Governor Dinwiddie.

"Glad to see you, Washington!" The governor greeted him with cordiality that surprised young George. "Stay to dinner. I want to hear about your brother and the voyage."

"Thank you, sir," George replied. "You honor me."

The elegance of the palace impressed George; it was even more beautiful than Belvoir. He saw that the governor lived well; he had a paunch and double chin. The man must be sixty—really old, George thought.

The governor sized George up, too; a promising young man, broad-shouldered and six feet two inches in height. After months of anxiety about Lawrence and his own illness, George probably looked more mature than his years—not quite twenty.

The governor was good company and the next morning George continued his journey to Mount Vernon. He rode a hired horse part way and for the rest of the hundred and fifty miles he hitchhiked with wagoners.

Nancy was thrilled to see George and have news of Lawrence. But she was distressed that her husband was not improving. George delivered Lawrence's letters to various neighbors and attended to many matters on the plantation, before he went on with his own work. In March he was out surveying in the Valley; he bought a tract of 552 acres of good land for a hundred and fifteen pounds.

During this spring after he was twenty, George decided to try for the office of Military Adjutant of Virginia. Lawrence still held that honor but he planned to resign. George had no military experience but in the nearly ten years that Lawrence held the job his younger brother had picked up some knowledge of the enlisting and training of the colony's militia. And the title and salary would satisfy his ambition to follow in Lawrence's steps.

That spring, too, George was worried by sad letters from Lawrence: he was in Bermuda; then he was worse and sailing home. He arrived in June and when they helped him from the ship, George and Nancy knew he could not live long. George again laid aside his own work and gave all his time and thought to Lawrence and his business.

"You are a great comfort to me, George," the sick man often said. "You know just what I like and how I want the plantation run."

Late in July, Lawrence died. He had appointed George one of six executors and as George was the only one who knew Lawrence's affairs, much depended on him. Lawrence's will divided his lands and businesses among Nancy, baby Sarah,

Austin, and George. Nancy was to have Mount Vernon for her lifetime, and then it was to be Sarah's. But if Sarah died without heirs, George was to have it. Legal inventories and details took many weeks.

George was still occupied with Lawrence's affairs when word came that the governor had appointed not one, but four adjutants. Virginia was bigger, he had decided; frontier dangers might make the work too much for one man. Well-known gentlemen were given the three desirable districts; George was appointed to a remote section below the James River. He was quite chagrined.

To be sure, he comforted himself, he was now a major— and he had a salary of one hundred pounds a year. Then he noticed that William Fitzhugh of Maryland had been given the Northern Neck district. Did Fitzhugh really want to serve?

"I shall apply for it, just in case," George decided. He did so when he took his oath of office. He got the job he wanted a year later. *That* was really a thrill!

Three weeks after he became a major, George celebrated his twenty-first birthday. There was an odd circumstance about this day. When he was born the "Old Calendar" was in use and the date was February eleventh. In 1752 England accepted the "New Style Calendar," and all dates after September 2, 1752 were put eleven days ahead. So when George was twenty-one he had a choice of dates for his birthday— February eleventh or twenty-second. Usually he chose to celebrate on the "Old Style" date. It seemed more his own day.

George took stock of himself on his coming of age. He owned 4,291 acres of debt-free land, about half of this bought with his own earnings. This land was not productive of income. His mother continued to use his inherited property; land in the Valley was bought for speculation. He rented some acreage, but the usual custom was to give a tenant farmer two years to clear land and put up buildings. After that the owner was to have rent in tobacco.

His father had held slaves, and George had inherited his share of these. But less than half were able-bodied—an owner must care for the aged and the young—and they worked on his inherited land. He owned his share of sheep and cattle at Ferry farm and horses he used for traveling. George's profession and his hope of profits in land were his most useful assets.

Other young men of his age in Virginia were still in England, being educated, or were reading law with some attorney. If they did not care for studies, they shared in the overseeing of the family plantation and enjoyed social pleasures.

George, like Lawrence, was more ambitious. He added to his meager schooling by reading and study and was now teaching himself military tactics so he could be a good adjutant. George had other personal assets. He carried himself well and made friends easily. He was a good marksman, a fine dancer, and one of the best horsemen in Virginia. And he had trained himself to endure cold and discomforts. All this made George seem more mature than most young men of his age.

That spring after George was twenty-one, he noticed that

men brought new facts when they came from far up the Potomac. He heard that Duquesne, the French governor, had sent troops to the south shore of Lake Erie. Indians, too, were there. Men in a little inn gathered around a messenger who said that the French were building a fort at the headwaters of the Ohio River.

"Look at those French," a trader said. "They build a fort and claim land for their king."

"England lets us open trade," another complained, "and then she claims all the land." His partner laughed cynically.

"Countries play tit for tat like youngsters," the host remarked to George, who was listening carefully. "Each tries to outsmart the other."

"That's all old country business," another said. "We're after the fur trade."

"Well you've got to have the Indians with you for that," a trader reminded them. "With both sides bribing redskins you don't know where you stand."

"I know," snorted his partner. "They wait and back the winner." Talk always ended on an uneasy note.

News of this sort prompted the governor to write to England for instructions. In August a letter informed Dinwiddie that the king was ordering all colonial governors to tell the French to return to Canada; force was to be used if necessary. All this was printed in the *Virginia Gazette,* a weekly paper published in Williamsburg. George chanced to see a copy in the fall while he was still out surveying.

"Tell the French." The phrase stayed in his mind. Men had said the French were near Lake Erie. How would Dinwiddie, in Williamsburg, "tell the French"? By messenger? But what messenger? No one in the capital had been as far north as George had gone—and he had not been within hundreds of miles of the rumored fort. George decided to go home (he still lived at Mount Vernon when not surveying) and see if Colonel Fairfax had news.

"I doubt if the governor has found a man to go," Fairfax guessed. "It will be a hard journey; few would want the task."

"I would like to offer my services," George said, and when Fairfax showed surprise he added, "I like adventure. I would like the chance to serve the colony—and the king." He stayed only long enough to get a meal and a fresh mount. Then he hurried on to Williamsburg.

The town was astir; horses pawed at hitchingracks; men talked at street corners. Raleigh Tavern was crowded and a stagecoach was bringing more guests. George went to the

palace, saw the governor and made his offer to act as messenger.

"Done!" Dinwiddie exclaimed. George saw that he was pleased to have a volunteer. They drove to the capitol to draft the message.

Soon George was called into the council chamber.

"You have two objectives," the governor said. "Go to Logstown—it's the English outpost on the Ohio—and renew friendship with the Indians. Then carry my letter to the French commandant, and bring back his reply." As he left the room with George the governor added, "I've written this second letter to Christopher Gist, asking him to go with you. Get all information you can about both Indians and the French. But above all, Major, make speed!"

As Washington turned away that word speed echoed in his mind. Speed—and this was late October, with the rainy season due to bring swollen rivers and treacherous trails.

Again George kept a diary and the entry for October 31st was: ". . . I arrived at *Fredericksburg,* and engaged Mr. *Jacob Vanbraam,* to be my *French* interpreter; and proceeded with him to *Alexandria,* where we provided Necessaries. From thence we went to *Winchester,* and got Baggage, Horses, &c; and . . . thence . . . to *Wills Creek.* . ." There they met Gist and with four helpers they set out northwest in a pouring rain. They had gone eight miles when a messenger overtook them.

"Your son is ill, Gist!" he shouted. "You must return!"

"What shall I do, Major?" Gist asked anxiously. "No one else has either medicine or skill to use it."

"Send back the medicine and instructions," Washington said. "You cannot return. You are guiding a mission for the colony."

The men watched George coldly. But George's steely-blue eyes and stern expression suggested no compromise. They already knew that he would be as firm with himself as with Gist. They held a blanket as protection from the rain while Gist measured medicine and wrote directions. The messenger started back, and the journey proceeded.

Up and over the mountains the party went on, slipping, sliding, drenched with cold rain. At Turtle Creek by the Monongahela they came to John Frazier's trading post. His news of the Indians was not reassuring. Three tribes had joined with the French.

"You'll likely find Half-King at Logstown," Frazier said and when George looked surprised he added, "He's a Seneca chief. His name is Tanacharisson but we call him Half-King because he owes allegiance to the Six Nations. I believe he's loyal to the English."

Frazier loaned them a canoe to save the horses part of the load. As George rode off, Frazier called, "Get John Davison if he's around. He talks every Indian dialect you'll need." Frazier and Davison and some three hundred other traders were men of the wilderness.

When they came to the point overlooking the union of the Monongahela and the Allegheny, George paused to study the place. It would be a good location for a fort.

"Guns here would command both rivers—and the Ohio," he said to Gist.

But they dared not stop. They swam horses across the river, joined the canoe party, and went on to Logstown.

This wilderness amazed George. Walnut and oak trees reared high, branches interlocked. Underfoot the trail was springy with the fallen leaves of centuries.

Davison was at Logstown and Half-King was nearby so a meeting was arranged for the next day. George now had his first experience with Indian ways.

The Indians, frontiersmen, and Washington's party met in the great "long house." Indians were in full regalia, others in frontier outfits—hip-length fur leggings, fur caps, boots, and coats. Half-King told of his interview with the French commandant.

"I told the French," Half-King said (and Davison translated), " 'This is our land. If you come peaceably, we will trade . . . but you build houses. You make forts.' " This was the heart of the Indian fears. " 'So fathers I ask you to withdraw.' " His glance indicated that he meant the English, too.

Then he raged on: "That Frenchman said, 'I am not afraid of flies . . . Indians are such as these! Down the river I will go. . . Here is your Wampum! I fling it at you!' "

After the drama the Indians agreed to guide George to the French at Venango, sixty miles north. But the commandant was not there. So George and his party traveled a

Guided by the Indians, George and his party traveled a hundred miles more to a fort called Le Boeuf, near Lake Erie.

hundred miles more to a fort called Le Boeuf, near Lake Erie. There they were greeted by the commandant, de St. Pierre, who promised to read Dinwiddie's letter the next day.

When they were alone, George said to his men:

"I was ordered to get information, so notice all you see. Van Braam, listen to the talk. Later I shall write it down."

In a couple of days the commandant conferred with George. "Your governor says this land belongs to Great Britain and asks us to leave. We are soldiers, under orders as you are, Major. You should go to Canada and see the governor."

"I have no orders to go to Canada," George answered, through Van Braam. So the commandant gave him a letter for Dinwiddie.

George was eager to leave; five hundred and sixty cold wet miles lay between him and Williamsburg. But he found that the Indians wanted to stay and that his horses were all but starved. To lighten the load, George accepted a canoe and with Gist paddled off. At least they had started.

They met the overland party but the horses were in such bad shape that George decided he and Gist would walk ahead to Frazier's. For men used to riding, the journey was a nightmare of sore feet, bitter cold, and danger from Indians.

At last they came to Frazier's where they dried out, had some hot food, and got horses to take them to Wills Creek.

"Speed!" Dinwiddie had said that sunny October day. George did his best. But it was the fifteenth of January of 1754 when at last he rode into Williamsburg.

...rised to find the streets ...rowded with excited men. But his c... ...He stabled his horse and hurried to the palace to deliver de St. Pierre's message to the governor. Dinwiddie waved him to a chair and opened the letter.

When he had finished, the governor turned to George.

"Now tell me everything!" he commanded.

"The French seem to think that the lands of the Ohio belong to them," George began. "I talked with men and with officers, sir. They claim that we are the intruders."

Dinwiddie snorted but said, "Go on!"

"They plan to occupy the land around the Ohio River in the spring," George said. "If we are to stop them we must act now."

The governor thoughtfully twisted a button on his coat.

"Go on," he repeated, and listened without comment as George recounted the highlights of the journey.

"You took notes, didn't you, Major?" he remarked as Washington paused. "I shall need a written report to present to the council tomorrow."

"Tomorrow!" Washington was dismayed. "I have only

rough notes, sir. To write a proper report will take some time."

"We have no time—you say so yourself, Major. We must act. Fortunately I have already sent Colonel Trent and some men with orders to build a fort. Perhaps you met him?"

"I passed him above Winchester," Washington replied. "I paused only to answer his questions about a suitable location for the fort. I advised the point where the rivers meet. Then I hurried on to you, sir."

"As you should," Dinwiddie approved.

Washington went to his room at the tavern, had some food sent in, and began studying his notes. By the next morning he had written about seven thousand words, which he took to the governor. While it was being read, George got breakfast and caught up on town news.

He learned that the governor and the council were in the midst of a quarrel about money, and that Dinwiddie had called the house of burgesses into session. This body had been created in 1619, while the capital of Virginia was in Jamestown. Two delegates, called burgesses, were elected from each of eleven large plantations; their duty was to establish a college and schools. The burgesses served under a council and the governor, appointed in London. By the time the capital was moved to Williamsburg in 1699, the burgesses had taken on considerable authority. They were growing more independent each decade.

At Raleigh Tavern Washington heard amazing talk. He realized that the quarrel with the governor was bitter when one man said boldly, "Dinwiddie thinks we'll back him up!

The governor's due for a jolt when the assembly votes!"

The laughter that followed gave George a new thought. Did Dinwiddie hope that threat of an attack by the French would divert attention from the dispute?

Five days later the council voted authority to Washington as adjutant of the Northern Neck to raise a company of one hundred men to stop the French advance. They also voted that Colonel Trent was to raise a company of one hundred frontiersmen. Washington's report was getting results.

As soon as he could get it printed, Dinwiddie had copies of George's report sent to the governors of all the other colonies and to London. It was published in newspapers and widely read. Probably this was the first time that the name of the twenty-two-year-old Virginian, George Washington, was known outside his own colony.

But all of this failed to make the burgesses less independent. They voted fifteen pounds to Washington for his expenses; not much, but still approval. They flatly refused the governor's request to send delegates to Albany to an inter-colony council for mutual defense. They voted ten thousand pounds of Virginia money for military use, but they put it under the control of a special committee. The governor could not touch it.

Dinwiddie was furious. He wrote to a friend, ". . . I am sorry to find them [the burgesses] very much in the republican way of thinking . . . I fear it will be difficult to bring them to order."

George was glad to leave the wrangles of Williamsburg

for his own work in Alexandria. This seaport town had been growing rapidly. Houses of brick looked substantial; often a shop was on the first floor and the family lived above in the second and third stories. Ships were building there, too, and Scottish shipwrights and ropemakers had moved in.

Washington drilled his troop daily on the Market Square in the center of town; just behind were the jail, whipping post, and stocks, warnings that citizens should obey the law.

Soon word came that the burgesses authorized six companies—Washington had not been able to recruit even *one!* They appointed Colonel Fry in command and Washington as lieutenant-colonel under him. Fry had worked with Peter Jefferson and knew the wilderness. Washington was pleased to serve under him. Major Muse was called to service, too; he was the only adjutant with war experience.

Washington's pride in his command was shaken when he learned that his pay was less than Dinwiddie had promised. He rode to Belvoir to talk with Colonel Fairfax.

"My feeling for justice, as well as my pride, is hurt," George said. "Officers in our army should be paid the same as those in the royal forces. I shall resign in protest."

"Someone has blundered," Fairfax said, with sympathy.

"My resigning will bring the error to light," George said.

"No, keep on with your task, George. I shall write to the governor. I shall urge him to raise colonial pay." With that promise George consented to return to Alexandria.

There he had trouble getting recruits and supplies. After

all his efforts, he had but seventy-five men. The governor promised a bonus of land near the new fort, but men were not interested in moving into the wilderness. As for supplies, thrifty merchants would not sell for government promises, and George had little cash.

"We shall have to start soon, if we are to surprise the French," Washington remarked to an aide after a day's drill.

"But the men haven't shoes or shirts, sir!" the man cried.

"I know," George answered, "But we must start in April."

"Royal troops were to join us," the aide said.

"So the governor said. But we cannot wait."

On the second of April, 1754, Washington and a hundred and twenty men left Alexandria for the northwest. With him were an army surgeon, Dr. James Craik of Alexandria, a drummer boy, and two creaking wagons of supplies. Townspeople cheered and the drummer boy beat his sticks as the proud little army marched away.

In a fortnight, they came to Winchester, ninety-seven miles on their way. Forty men joined up with them there and the journey continued, over mountains, through deep forests.

They had gone about a hundred miles, half the planned journey, when word came that the French had taken Colonel Trent's half-built fort. Trent and his men were allowed to retreat on their promise not to return to the Ohio area.

"The French have a thousand men!" the messenger shouted. "They have the best equipment!" This was bad news, indeed.

Washington hurried a report off to Dinwiddie. Then he wrote directly to the governors of Pennsylvania and Maryland, asking for help—a bold stroke for a young officer. That done, he took council with his men. The danger was plain, but they voted to go forward. A fort at Redstone Creek was needed; they pushed westward, building a road as they went.

The weather moderated, though ice still fringed the creeks in the morning. Trees budded and songbirds, like gay flowers, perched on the branches. Men felled trees, hunted fords, filled marshes.

They were building a crude bridge over the Youghiogany when a messenger from Half-King brought news: French scouts were in the neighborhood. Minutes later a second messenger arrived; the French were fifteen miles away and would attack on sight. Washington followed the two messengers to confer with Half-King.

"The French are bold; Indians like that," Half-King said. "But I am with the English. You protect my people; I join you in battle."

This promise encouraged Washington to continue to build that fort. But the men were uneasy. They watched the forest, imagining they saw French uniforms behind every tree.

On a balmy day in late May, they came to a wide meadow, quiet and beautiful in the sunshine. The peaceful illusion was quickly shattered by a breathless messenger.

"The French are hiding over there!" He jerked a nervous thumb over his shoulder. "They're ready to attack!"

"We shall fortify ourselves here," Washington decided. "This is a good place." In his inexperience, Washington did not realize that open ground surrounded by forest was the worst of all spots for defense. He had the men cut brush and dig trenches; he spoke of the place as Fort Necessity.

Meanwhile, he sent out scouts to locate the French and thus guard against a surprise attack. Next evening another messenger came with news that Washington wrote of later:

"I received an express from the Half-King . . . he had seen tracks of two men which he had followed to an obscure place; he was of the opinion that the whole party of the French was hidden there. . . [We] set out in a heavy rain, and in night as dark as pitch, along a path scarce broad enough for one man. . . All night we continued. . ."

Near dawn they reached the Indian camp, talked with Half-King, and decided to attack together. Washington placed his men on one side of a little valley; the Indians took the other slope. They were barely in position when they heard the alarm.

Firing began and lasted about fifteen minutes. The action was a relief—and a danger. Ten French soldiers were killed, among them the leader, Jumonville; twenty-one were taken prisoner; and one got away. Were more French troops near? Washington did not know. He took his men and the prisoners back to the little fort.

Gist was there with news. Colonel Fry had been thrown from a horse and had died of his injuries. Washington was appointed acting field-officer in charge of the expedition. Fate had given the young officer a grave responsibility.

"British regulars are coming," Gist told Washington, "about a hundred men under Captain Mackay."

This, as it turned out, was not good news. The regulars would not work at road making; *they* were the King's troops. They stood idly watching while the colonials, poorly dressed and paid a third as much, toiled with rocks and tree stumps. Worse still, Mackay would take no orders from Washington. To save the peace, Washington decided to get on with that road to Redstone Creek. As they were leaving, Major Muse arrived, with the remnant of Fry's men. Being colonials, they would help with the road. Washington took them along.

As he worked with the men, Washington saw that he could not make the swift stroke he had planned; he lacked both men and supplies. The Indians were unreliable; his men were weak with hunger. The French were advancing.

"What shall I do, Half-King?" he asked. The chief had stayed with the Virginians. "Shall we go on? Or take a stand here? Or retreat and make a more effective battle later?"

"Retreat!" Half-King was horrified. "Desert us? *Cowards!*" He spat out the word. Washington needed no interpreter to understand his scorn.

"We are no longer your friends!" Half-King shouted. The Indians vanished into the forest.

Washington decided to return to the fort; so the Virginians began the miserable trek back over the road newly hacked out of the forest. There was not enough food. The ground was sodden, and cannon must be dragged by hungry men. When they got to Fort Necessity, they hardly had strength to improve the fortifications.

Rain was pouring down on the third of July when, near midday, a shot sounded—the French had come! The fort in a meadow gave attackers every advantage; they fired from behind trees. Drenched with rain, the Virginians stood in mud under deadly cross-fire.

"Fire, man!" Washington shouted to a soldier whose musket lay idle on his knees. "What're you quitting for?"

"How kin I fire?" the man asked his commander angrily. "My powder's nothing but wet paste!"

In the evening the French commander called a parley and offered surrender terms, written in French. Van Braam, George's companion at Fort le Boeuf, was the only one with him who could read French. Even he had trouble: the paper was wet, the light faint and flickering.

"We are to give up arms," he read. Washington objected.

"Impossible! We need those as protection against the Indians!" The French officer agreed that this was fair enough.

Van Braam continued reading and translating. Two Virginians were to be left as hostages until men taken prisoners earlier were returned. Washington chose Van Braam and Strobo for this. Then Mackay, Washington, and the French officers signed.

The next morning the retreat began. About three miles

from Fort Necessity the English and Virginians stopped to check their numbers and to rest. Casualties were thirteen dead and fifty-four wounded, some too badly to be moved. A few men were left to care for these and the rest, less than three hundred, went on.

While the roll was being checked, Washington and Captain Mackay studied the surrender paper. In daylight they could read some letters, but no words of the French.

"Can you make anything of this?" Mackay asked one of his aides. "You read some French, don't you?"

The man studied the paper. "You signed a confession that you assassinated Jumonville!" he cried.

Washington took the paper; his hand was shaking.

"Van Braam read nothing about that!" cried Mackay.

"He read a sentence about the 'death' or 'loss' of Jumonville," Washington said.

"But here it is, twice—the paper is a signed confession." The man pointed out the words. *"L'assassin"* did look like "assassinate," Washington admitted; but they had not intended a confession of what was not true. Washington put the paper away with others he was taking to the governor.

The next morning, July 4, 1754, the troops moved on.

That retreat was a dreadful experience for the ambitious young commander. He had lost men and supplies; the surrender paper was a deep worry. But worst of all for Washington was the knowledge that he had failed. The French now held the Ohio country.

Braddock
and the Wilderness

As soon as his troops were encamped at Wills Creek, Washington left to face the governor and the Council. A messenger had already taken south his report and the surrender paper.

The nearly three-hundred-mile journey gave the commander time to think over his situation. The location of the fort was a mistake. But lack of supplies and men, and insufficient royal support contributed to failure. Would Dinwiddie realize that? And *what* would he say about that surrender paper?

To his astonishment, the assembly gave Washington a vote of thanks and to each soldier, one pistole. And they praised their efforts.

A few weeks later, Washington's supposed "confession" to the killing of Jumonville was published in France. That version said that Jumonville and his men were on a peaceful mission like Washington's trip to Fort le Boeuf. The French account made further trouble between England and France.

But Virginians gave little heed to the affair. Some blamed Van Braam and thought he was a traitor. Washington was thought to have done his best to protect the colony.

However, Washington hardly had time to enjoy his relief when other unpleasant matters turned up. Dinwiddie refused to return the French prisoners, an affront to the signed agreement. George was further affronted when he learned that colonial troops were reassigned and their officers demoted.

"If I go back to Wills Creek," George said to a friend, "I shall be a captain under Colonel Innes. I am a lieutenant-colonel."

The friend saw that George was losing his temper so he said smoothly, "Innes is a great friend of Dinwiddie."

"Well, I am the governor's friend and I work for the good of Virginia," George retorted hotly. "But it is *not* for the good of the colony to have royal troops better fed, clothed and paid —and rank over colonials. I shall resign!" He turned in his commission.

Brilliant autumn foliage was fading when he started north from Williamsburg in November of 1754. As his temper cooled his thoughts turned from colony affairs to his own future. Washington was nearing twenty-three and passing years had brought many changes in the Washington family.

Betty Washington was now Mrs. Fielding Lewis of Kenmore, Fredericksburg. Betty and George were fond of each other; he often stayed at her house on his journeys. His brothers were all married and lived in the Tidewater country. Their mother continued to manage Ferry farm though it belonged to George. He approved her staying there but he would have enjoyed managing the place. She would expect him home,

now. The role of a dutiful son would be hard for a young man who had developed independence and leadership. But no other land he owned had a suitable house.

Thoughts turned to his beloved half-brother; nearly two and a half years had passed since Lawrence died. Nancy had followed the custom of the time and promptly remarried. As Mrs. George Lee she lived on her husband's plantation in Westmoreland. Baby Sarah had died. George thought of Mount Vernon, empty now. Would Nancy rent the place to him?

He rode over and found Mount Vernon much neglected. Indoors the empty house echoed coldly. He wandered through the rooms to the study—and there stopped short. On the wall was the familiar oil portrait of Lawrence; the red coat with gilt braid seemed to brighten the whole room. A tricorne hat was tucked under his left arm in a characteristic gesture.

George stood before the picture, his heart beating fast. The portrait made Lawrence seem close; George remembered the fun they had had when it was painted. Across from the portrait was another memento—Lawrence's commission of 1740 as "Captain in a Regiment of Foot to be raised in America." Nancy had left these things for him! George was determined, now, to live at Mount Vernon.

Nancy was willing to rent for fifteen thousand pounds of tobacco a year; a high rental, but George thought by hard work he could pay it and put the place in good shape.

The house was modest, but large for a bachelor. Nancy,

of course, had taken her furniture; he must replace that. Even though the house was empty, George was happier than he had been for months. When Governor Sharpe of Maryland offered him a place on his staff—a real honor—George declined, almost casually.

George Washington soon fitted into the gay life of the neighborhood. A tall handsome man, well thought of in the colony, who rode as well as he danced, was a welcome guest. The Fairfaxes gave a party for him, and men lingered at the table, discussing colonial business while the ladies primped for the dancing to follow.

"Have you had time to read the latest Gazette?" George William Fairfax asked Washington at the table. "It says Dinwiddie is joining with Sharpe to throw out the French and boost English prestige."

"Is that why a new fort—Cumberland, I hear they call it —is being built near Wills Creek?" a voice down the table asked.

"I have read of it," Washington replied. "That should be a good spot for a fort—the gateway to the mountains."

"Dinwiddie has called a conference with the Indians," a Williamsburg man remarked. "He wants troops from England; claimed he knew the French were sending more troops."

"Those in greatest danger are the settlers," Washington said with deep feeling. "Indians massacre and terrorize. If something is not done to stop them, the settlers—those that are left alive—will move back east." But talk of settlers meant little to men who had never slept in a rough frontier cabin. "Indians are caught between us and the French," George went on. "They lose, whichever nation wins." Men shook their heads, puzzled by that statement.

"We are not a military people," Fairfax said. "I hope the governor doesn't go too far. Come, gentlemen, shall we join the ladies?"

Into this rural scene a new note intruded early in 1755. General Edward Braddock with royal troops arrived off the Virginia Capes; his coming was part of an overall plan to take every French fort in America. His two frigates sailed up the Potomac, passed Mount Vernon, colors flying, and anchored at Alexandria.

Braddock himself lingered at Williamsburg to confer with the governor. The general was short, stout, and sixty, and well trained in the European style of war. He was not optimistic about this American campaign; word his scouts brought did not please him.

"Your colonial army is small and lacks supplies," Braddock complained to a group entertaining him at the tavern. "And I hear that your wilderness is appalling," he went on. "My scouts tell me that you have not even one good road."

"Not yet, General," someone murmured, amused. All this had been written in letters to England, but had not been believed.

When the general dined at the palace, later, Dinwiddie tried to smooth matters over. "You will find, General, that

America differs from England. Here we have mountains, Indians—"

"But have you no one who knows conditions and could go
with me?" Braddock interrupted. "If conditions are so different, I surely need an experienced colonial on my staff!"

"Well," Dinwiddie paused, thinking, "actually I do have
such a man—or rather, I did have him. Young George Washington has had both military and wilderness experience. But
he is hotheaded and proud. We quarreled." He told the general about the difficulties of rank and pay.

"I can get around that young man," Braddock replied. "I
shall invite him to be a guest member of my personal staff—
the royal army staff. Then the question of rank will not arise."

That settled, the governor and the general made plans for
a meeting of the governors of Pennsylvania, New York, Maryland, Massachusetts, and Virginia in mid-April, to plan for the
campaign.

Meanwhile George had ridden to Alexandria. He was
fascinated by the changes the troops had made. The regulars
were in camp northwest of town; they walked the streets in
handsome red coats, well fed, well drilled. Smart British officers swaggered about before respectful townsfolk.

Small boys, their eyes popping, called the regulars "redcoats"; and the British, once they saw the shortcoats the colonial
soldiers wore, retorted by calling them "bobtails."

It was a stirring scene and George had a pang as he returned to his fields. Had he made a mistake to resign?

He was busy with planting, though still half regretful, when the invitation came to join Braddock's staff. Washington was flabbergasted. He thought of Alexandria and the stirring scenes now enacted there; of his status as a colonial; of the tobacco that must be planted and tended to pay the rent. He thought of Fort Necessity: that defeat rankled. If he was with Braddock and helped to take Fort Duquesne the score would be evened. He rode to Alexandria to see Braddock.

The general introduced George to members of his staff, attractive young men near George's own age. He took a liking to William Shirley, son of the Massachusetts governor.

"You should join us," Shirley said. "The governors will be here soon and life will be gay. We shall have stirring times ahead in the campaign, too."

"I should like to share such a program," Washington's eyes were amused as well as pleased. He knew Alexandria would be gay but he also knew, more than Shirley, some features of the campaign.

George called on Braddock and talked to him frankly.

"I should like to go with you, sir. But I must make arrangements for my plantation."

"Of course," Braddock agreed. "Come as soon as you can."

George rode home and sent for his brother Jack. The youth was only twenty, but trustworthy. He came at once and took over the plans George had made for the season.

In Alexandria the governors and their staffs were arriving by coach. Every tavern was packed; the governors were entertained in private houses such as the Carlyles', where Sarah Fair-fax was hostess. On the market square bobtails drilled early and late. Drummers of the colonials vied with those of the redcoats. Men came and went from ships lying at the wharf.

Governors dined and danced evenings and by day carried on their serious business in a room at John Carlyle's. They voted to tax all the colonies for the war England was making against the French in America. This seemingly logical act was un-popular and proved to be the first step in a long series of events that ended with severing of all ties with England.

A week after the governors' meeting the redcoats and bob-tails departed for Fort Cumberland. Even before they arrived, frictions began. Braddock was careless about Indians and had no presents for them. He disagreed with Washington about transport; George advised packhorses because of the mountains. Braddock insisted on wagons. It was a relief when Braddock sent George to Williamsburg to fetch money to pay the troops.

Soon after that mission, George was very ill with some-thing like typhoid fever; he was barely able to be about when two thousand men left for Duquesne. But he went with them.

The rugged Alleghenies infuriated Braddock. His wagon transport broke down; cannons slid crashing into ravines. Often the troops made but two miles in a whole day.

"Could we leave some supplies?" George asked. Braddock was carrying full equipment for gentlemen soldiers. "We can never surprise the French at this pace. A rear guard could bring them up."

Braddock nodded, frowning. Then he noticed Washington's thin, white face. George had been riding in a jolting wagon. "Dr. Craik will not let you ride a horse yet."

"I shall keep with the rear guard," George replied, "and overtake you as soon as I am able. Promise me you will let me know before you attack the fort!"

Braddock promised and went ahead with twelve hundred men. The others, under Colonel Dunbar, second in command, were to follow with supplies as quickly as possible.

June passed. The forest, so terrifying in winter, was beautiful now. But Englishmen were used to a cool climate and felt smothered under mighty trees. Still they went on, daily coming nearer the French fort.

Washington joined the troops at the mouth of the Youghiogany river about fifteen miles from Fort Duquesne. This evening of July the eighth he found everyone in fine spirits.

"Victory is practically won!" Shirley greeted him.

"Give us one, maybe two, days more and we shall be standing in the fort, counting French prisoners," another aide said.

The ninth dawned, a perfect midsummer day, and the line got under way promptly. Washington was still weak, but he mounted his horse and rode with the staff.

Braddock had decided to cross the Monongahela river, march north a few miles and then reford the stream about nine miles from the fort. The first ford was crossed. As they splashed through the second Washington peered anxiously into the woods to the east. This, he saw, was a logical spot for a surprise attack.

"Never have I seen such a beautiful scene," he told himself trying for reassurance. The trees in summer glory, the sparkling water, the bright flags, the red coats of the English, the brilliant blue of the colonials were unforgettable. Martial music (in complete disregard of the enemy) gave a festive air to the line of marching men.

"Now would be the time," George thought and he felt a chill of apprehension in spite of the warm day.

With others of the staff he mounted the east bank. "That rise of ground just ahead . . ." he began, then stopped. Why tell them that the enemy could shoot directly on them? Nothing was happening.

Nothing? A shot shattered the day's peace. One shot— a dozen, a hundred. Then war whoops that chilled the bravest hearts. In seconds the march was a rout. Well-trained Britons saw Virginians seek shelter behind trees and followed.

"*Cowards!*" Braddock yelled bitterly, ashamed of his men. "Would you hide behind trees?" He galloped about with the greatest courage, rallying his men. Many obeyed from habit and their bright coats and solid formation made a perfect target for Indians and French hidden in ravines or behind trees.

Washington saw they would all be killed without a chance
for defense. Sudden strength flowed into him. He waved his
sword and plunged ahead.

"Shoot from safety, Virginians!" he yelled. "Keep firing!"

A dozen enemy muskets blazed at him from a ravine. A
bullet nipped his coat. Another shot down his horse.

"Watch out for yourself, George . . ." Washington heard
Shirley's voice and turned as his friend fell, instantly killed by
a bullet in his head. Washington threw his leg free as his own
horse fell, grabbed Shirley's mount, and rode on.

"Keep firing, Virginians!" Washington shouted again. A
rain of bullets fell and this horse, too, died under him. Washington rallied a group of foot soldiers while Braddock, clutching his side, dashed by, shouting orders.

The battle was short. Indians began taking scalps and the
English, seeing that attention was diverted, ran for the ford.
George grabbed the bridle of a riderless horse and flung him-
self onto the blood-spattered saddle to join the general.

Braddock was mortally injured. One of his aides unwound
his wine-colored sash and several helped to lift the general
onto it. Soldiers carried him by the strong fringe as on a litter
and hurried away. With frightened backward looks men ran

for their lives. Soon the survivors had crossed the second ford. Of the twelve hundred men who had marched that morning, nine hundred were killed or taken prisoner. Braddock knew that he was dying. He sent for Washington.

"My hunch was right," he said with a wan smile. "This mission was not marked for success. I have never seen such fighting. I did not believe the tales I had heard of Indian battle." He stopped for breath a moment.

"Go at once," he ordered. "Fetch relief and provisions. I was so sure we would be in the fort—we have no food, none!"

Washington stiffened. Sheer will power gave him strength to dash off to Dunbar and the rear guard. But when Washington met that frightened officer, Dunbar would give no help. He destroyed needed supplies and hurried off to safety.

The next day the feeble remnant of Braddock's army came to the place Dunbar had deserted. The sight of wasted food and powder infuriated the hungry men—but Dunbar was gone.

Braddock died on the fourth day, knowing the full bitterness of defeat. Washington read the burial service as his body was lowered into a grave dug in the road. Later, wagons were driven over it to hide the grave from Indians hunting scalps. That much they could do for a brave man.

At Fort Duquesne, where the English were to have been celebrating victory, comrades who were taken prisoners were burned at the stake. Smoke from those torturing fires told the wilderness people that the English were beaten. As the savages celebrated, the French stood aside, silent, victorious.

The War Drags On

"So this is the way I wipe out the disgrace of Fort Necessity!" George's thoughts were bitter as he gathered up the few supplies Dunbar had left and led the troops back to Fort Cumberland. Reaction from strain while still weak made his depression worse.

The soldiers watched him with admiration. Many officers had been killed; Dunbar had made off as soon as he knew of the defeat. What would they have done but for this young Virginian?

When they reached Fort Cumberland, Washington had the hard task of writing the bad news to Dinwiddie. His letter ended:

"I tremble at the consequences that this defeat will have on our back settlers, who, I suppose, will all leave their habitations unless . . . measures are taken for their security."

The express messenger delivered the report to the palace, then hurried along the green to the Duke of Gloucester Street. A crowd quickly gathered to hear his news.

"Braddock defeated!" The word spread like fire.

"Braddock had the regulars!" a man cried. "Best troops ever in Virginia! Saw 'em with my own eyes!"

"Braddock's dead," the messenger said, making the most of his bit of limelight. "All the officers dead, I reckon. Except Colonel Washington. He brought us back to Fort Cumberland. Stayed right with us though he was sick—lucky if he pulls through. That Dunbar—he hurried to Philadelphia to save himself, I heard."

News spread to the bake shop, the wigmaker's, the taverns, and picked up drama in each retelling. Men who had looked on Braddock with awe in the spring now blamed him for the tragedy. Some said the colony should have depended on Colonel Washington, the hero today.

Washington was astonished to receive letters of extravagant praise of his courage and daring. Some wrote to his brothers, mourning his death. Jack wrote asking a soldier friend for facts. George replied at once that he was alive, indeed. He wrote to Austin, too. ". . . the defeat was so scandalous that I hate to have it mentioned." Then he summed up his military service since his first journey into the wilderness.

"I was employed to go on a journey in winter . . . and got my expenses paid. I was appointed with trifling pay to conduct a handful of men to the Ohio. What did I get by this? . . . My command reduced . . . I have always been on the loosing order ever since I entered the service . . . I am always ready . . . to do my country any service I am capable of but never upon the terms I have done." By "my country" he meant Virginia.

After he sent those letters, Washington was again ill—a relapse of his fever. He was tenderly nursed by Thomas Bishop.

This man had been Braddock's servant and was employed by Washington at the dying general's request. When Washington was able to travel, the two went south to Mount Vernon.

At home, George pondered on his share in the defeat. He had advised against wagons, preferring pack horses; he had tried to tell Braddock about Indian fighting. The general would not listen to either suggestion. George had urged dividing the troops for speedier attack—had that advice caused defeat?

Letters and visitors showed George that instead of being blamed, he was being praised for this last suggestion, which Braddock took. Soldiers wrote that Braddock's way of fighting, in solid ranks, would have lost any battle, and that Washington had saved all those who were bringing up supplies. His reputation grew steadily as men spoke of his courage in battle and wisdom afterward.

The Reverend Samuel Davies preached about "that heroic youth, Colonel George Washington, whom . . . Providence has preserved . . . for important service to his country."

Gist wrote from Philadelphia, "Your name is more talked of here than any other in the colony." Anger at Braddock's obstinacy and contempt for Dunbar helped to promote Washington's fame. Men demanded that he be made commander in chief of Virginia forces.

Washington did not enjoy this acclaim.

"People will expect too much," he said to Jack. "They will expect me to save them from Indians and the French."

"Someone needs to rescue the poor settlers from the Indians," Jack replied. "I heard frightful tales at Alexandria today. What has stirred them up, George?"

"Well, Half-King died. He was good as a go-between, though he was angry at us the last time I saw him," George answered. "Then Braddock hurt their pride; he never catered to the Indians. And since they have discovered that three hundred Indians and French could defeat twelve hundred royal troops in fifteen minutes, they have run wild. There will be no living settler in Virginia if they are not stopped soon."

"I heard in Alexandria that Braddock's new road is wide open," Jack complained. "They say Indians travel on it constantly, coming upon settlers, killing and taking prisoners."

In August, Dinwiddie obeyed the popular command and appointed Washington as commander. He sent the papers to Mount Vernon by messenger. This evidence of trust pleased George and seemed to complete his recovery, for he quickly rode off to Williamsburg. At the palace he talked with Dinwiddie.

"Before I can accept, sir," he said, "I must know that I shall have proper moneys for paying and equipping men. And good arrangements for supplies of food and equipment." Being asked for the job gave him bargaining power.

"Have no concern," Dinwiddie promised heartily. "We shall see to it that you have everything you need."

"Thank you, sir." Washington bowed, hoping the governor would keep his promise. "Then I shall sign." He reached for a quill and set his name on the document that gave him charge of all the militia in Virginia.

On his trip north, Washington visited Fredericksburg and Alexandria, seeing about enlistments. Then he went on to Winchester, which was to be his headquarters. This village was near Greenway Court, Lord Fairfax's estate; George knew the neighborhood well. He opened an office in a snug two-room cabin built of field stone. The narrow windows had shutters made of three thicknesses of wood, each cut on a different grain; neither bullets nor tomahawks would easily go through. By the door was a good well.

But the state of the militia was far from pleasing. Washington saw that his most important task was recruiting. Soldiers, and officers, too, felt little responsibility to the colony. Desertions were frequent, in spite of flogging or even hanging when the deserters were caught. Men were not inclined to risk scalping for the sake of settlers they had never seen.

Washington and his officers had little chance to be with the men: that was not the custom in that day. Contact was only with the petty officer, who might be a third-rate innkeeper or Indian trader who in turn wanted to protect his own scalp.

Sometimes when an alarm came in from a settler, a few brave men volunteered. Though they hurried, they usually arrived to find the cabin burned and the people dead or kidnapped. Such a scene was common as Washington rode about the country.

These trips around the country were to inspect small forts,

recruit men, or get food. Once he wrote a personal bond to buy 620 fine beeves; the owner had more faith in Washington's paper than in Virginia's.

"Now we must find some casks and salt to put that meat down for the winter," Washington planned as they rode away.

Scouts estimated that 150 Indians, in small groups, drove off or killed all the settlers within thirty miles of the fort. And this within three months of Braddock's defeat. It was a shocking record of misery and death.

On a late autumn day, Washington came back to Fort Cumberland and was annoyed to find that old problem of rank again—when he needed help for serious matters, too. Captain Dagworthy and thirty men had taken over the fort with three hundred colonials. The place was in a turmoil. Dagworthy had held a royal commission; he would give orders, but not take any.

Washington tried tact. He tried ignoring the man. Both failed, so he went to Williamsburg. Dinwiddie had promised him authority; now let him keep that pledge.

Colonel Washington was always a conspicuous man. He carried himself well and seemed even taller than his six-foot-two inches. He was welcomed by a crowd when he hitched his horse at the rack in front of Raleigh Tavern. Legislature was in session, and the town was lively after the long season of heat and flies.

The cordiality of the welcome surprised him, till he learned that magazines with accounts of the Braddock battle had just

come from England. The writer praised Virginia troops and Washington. He found himself a hero! This would be no help with the governor.

Dinwiddie, at the palace, had a slyly amused air when George told his story.

"You, the great Washington, the hero! You complain to me about one officer?" His fat paunch shook with laughter.

"But, sir," Washington protested, flushing hotly, "I have no authority over the man. I am a colonial. Only an officer of the king can settle Dagworthy."

"Ridiculous!" scoffed Dinwiddie. "But since you are not able to manage, I might write to Shirley." Governor Shirley was acting commander in chief of the British army in America.

George had to be content. Disgruntled, he left for the north. The route took Washington through Fredericksburg and Alexandria. Naturally he stopped by Mount Vernon to see how Jack was getting along with the farms. George had just handed his bridle to a stableman when Jack rode into the yard. They greeted each other with pleasure.

"I hope you have time to look over the books, George," Jack said. "I'm not as good with accounts as you are."

"I shall have to go on tomorrow," George replied. "We could do them now."

The cook spied the colonel and bustled about to make a fine dinner. A houseman hurried to make extra fires.

The brothers went into the study. George glanced at Lawrence's portrait; it was ever an inspiration to him. Then he

tackled the books Jack spread out on the desk. Jack watched him anxiously until he saw George relax.

"You have done well, Jack," his brother said warmly after awhile. "We are in better shape than I dared hope."

"It is not too bad, considering the dry season," Jack admitted. His face was flushed; praise sounded good. "Nancy has her rent; I have done the repairs you planned, and still some money is left."

"Enough for . . ." George began, but then paused. A new and dazzling idea has just come into his mind, but it needed thinking over. "Enough for comfort," he concluded. "You have done well, Jack."

As they ate supper Jack remarked, "Remember that Mr. Fairfax stands for election as burgess, George? He wishes you could come down and electioneer. He suspects there will be a contest."

"That will be in December." George was thoughtful. "Well, I might make it. Tell him that I shall try." The next morning George left early for his duties in Winchester.

Washington did come to help his friend on that December election day. After a lively contest Fairfax was elected. The colonel was astonished when he learned that his own name was written on forty ballots. Friends told him he should work for himself next time.

Dinwiddie's letter did not solve the problem of Dagworthy. So after the election, George pondered on the idea he had thought of while working with Jack. Why not travel to Boston and talk to Governor Shirley? He looked up distances: it would be about 1100 miles, but worth it if he got the business settled. Winter was the only time a colonel dared leave his duty; ice and snow guarded the mountain passes better than the soldiers.

"The governor will like to hear of his son's last day," George told himself. He remembered the kindly governor and how he had looked at the meeting in Alexandria.

The result was that in February of 1756, a party of five set out for Boston. With Washington were two young captains, George Mercer and Robert Stewart, as aides, and two servants, one the faithful Bishop.

They stopped in Philadelphia and bought new clothes. Then they went on to New York where they were lavishly entertained by former Virginians. Washington was attracted to pretty Mary Philipse, their host's sister-in-law. He squired her to the parties and promised to see her again.

The *Boston Gazette* had an article about the visitor. It referred to him as "the Hon. Col. Washington, a gentleman who has deservedly a high reputation for military skill and valor." And in due time the governor received him.

Shirley said Dagworthy should leave Fort Cumberland or "put himself under the command of Col. Washington." This seemed a victory, until George learned that Dagworthy's friend, Governor Sharpe, had power over all colonial troops.

"It is a petty thing," George told himself. But he felt an anger against royal privilege that was to rankle bitterly for years.

A New Life Emerges

For two whole years after the Boston journey, Washington had to fight a defensive war on a four-hundred-mile frontier. The string of small, poorly equipped forts suffered frequent surprise attack and each time, men deserted.

Washington wrote:

"... I am distracted what to do? ... Three families were murdered the night before last ... twelve miles from this place." Worse still, he discovered a plot in the fort itself to surrender to the French! And his forces were too weak to punish the traitors.

The colonel wrote for permission to attack Fort Duquesne. As long as Indians had that stronghold back of them, he explained, they would continue their cruelties.

"The French must have taken troops from Duquesne to fight elsewhere," George remarked to an aide as he sealed the letter. "Now is the time to attack." Later he was proved right.

The strain of frontier tragedies, hard riding and lack of rest broke even George's remarkable strength. He was seriously ill for four months as his twenty-fifth birthday approached. While he lay sick, Dinwiddie left for England, little regretted.

Francis Fauquier, a very different sort of man, came to take his place.

News of changes in England drifted to Mount Vernon, too. The new Prime Minister, William Pitt, had an understanding of colonial needs and promised to bring the war with the French to a victorious end. George had a letter that recounted how Pitt planned to wage active campaigns against three forts, Louisburg in the northeast, Ticonderoga, and Duquesne. George read the letter twice—but it did not say that a Virginia colonel was to have a command.

In March he decided to go to Williamsburg for medical advice; some army business needed attention, too. With Bishop, he started south, but was not able to gallop steadily as was his habit. He set a slow pace; stopped a time with his sister and at other places.

The two got to the ferry over the Pamunkey about dinner time one day. This wide river merges here with the Mattiponi to form the York River. Ferrying was tedious, but once across, a traveler had only about fifteen miles to Williamsburg. Washington's friend, Colonel Chamberlayne, lived near the ferry and often watched for friends who might be crossing over. He saw George and sent a servant to invite him to dinner.

"Tell the colonel I must push on," Washington told the man. "I plan to be in Williamsburg before dark. Assure him that I shall accept his invitation on my return journey."

"Colonel Chamberlayne will fret if I bring that message, sir," the servant protested. "He invites you *now*."

Such urging could not be refused. Washington dismounted and handed Bishop the bridle. "Wait here," he said, "I shall tell the colonel myself and thank him."

In the great hall Chamberlayne greeted George warmly and led him into the drawing room. There George saw a domestic scene that stopped him short and banished thought of travel. By a cheerful fire a pretty young woman sat, embroidering. Close by, two attractive children were playing contentedly. George was fascinated.

Before Chamberlayne could introduce him, Washington stepped forward and spoke to the lady. He had known Mr. and Mrs. Daniel Parke Custis in the fashionable circle in Williamsburg. Likely George had danced a minuet or reel with her in the Apollo Room at Raleigh Tavern, or in the handsome ballroom at the palace. He may even have been entertained at parties in their home, Six Chimneys, on Francis Street. Mr. Custis had died a year or more before this day.

For a few minutes they chatted. Then George stepped to the hall and called a servant. "Tell my man that I am staying for dinner," he ordered. "Horses are to be ready in an hour."

Washington saw that Martha Custis was small and dainty with glossy brown hair, dark eyes, and graceful figure. Women had little formal education in those days, but Martha had a winning manner and quick wit. And she was doubtless the richest heiress in Virginia.

Dinner over, Washington lingered. Outside in the dusk, horses pawed impatiently; Bishop could hardly hold them.

"Colonel Washington is staying overnight," a houseman finally came out to say. The astonished Bishop led the horses to the stable.

Next morning when they finally departed he overheard Washington tell Mrs. Custis that he would stop at her plantation, nearby, on his return journey. It was then that he got her promise to marry him when he was free to leave active service. Some time later the price of a lady's ring entered in his account book showed that their troth was properly pledged.

Three weeks later he got leave to ride south. He saw Martha and went to Mount Vernon. There he made plans with Jack about remodeling his house. A story-and-a-half house would be too small for his new family. To enlarge it, he added one story—making it two-and-a-half stories and keeping the dormer windows on what would be the third floor. He also planned to decorate and clean the whole house. Jack promised to start the work at once.

Winchester was astir when Washington arrived there after an absence of five months. The road between Fort Cumberland and the village where he had had his headquarters was widened, and transport came and went continually. Brigadier-General John Forbes, a Scot, was appointed by Pitt to direct the campaign against Fort Duquesne.

"Forbes has twelve hundred Highlanders," a captain told Washington. "Best trained men you ever saw."

"They're enlisting men from Pennsylvania, Maryland, and Virginia—claim they'll have five thousand soon," another said.

"Five thousand!" George exclaimed, incredulously.

"Right," the captain nodded. "They plan for two thousand Virginians. Wouldn't wonder but they get 'em, too. Forbes is good."

At first, George had felt put out—*he* had been commander in chief here, not so long before. Now royal troops were taking over. But the more he heard of Forbes the more he wished to serve under him. He had never had such a good chance to learn tactics. So he wrote letters and let it be known that he wanted an assignment. He was given command of a regiment of Virginia infantry and worked hard getting his troops into top shape.

Then to Washington's dismay, the question of what route to take to the fort came up. Pennsylvanians had convinced Forbes that the best route should go northeast to the little town of Raystown, Pennsylvania, then straight west.

"Can't the general see that the Pennsylvanians are talking only for themselves!" George exclaimed when he heard the news.

A young officer chuckled. "The Pennsies are talkers. And it *is* a good road for them, Colonel."

"Hasn't he scouts to tell him about the land?" George asked.

"General Forbes is a good military man," the officer said. "But he knows no more about the American mountain wilderness than Braddock did. I ought to know. I served with both. Try talking to him yourself if you don't believe."

Washington did just that. At the first opportunity he spoke to the general, frankly and politely.

"This route through Raystown," he said, "will be much longer in the making. It covers more miles; it must all be newly made. Braddock's road is three years old and no doubt overgrown. But the great trees are down at least; repairs would not take long."

Forbes looked around the landscape dubiously. The rolling hills seemed fine country. Why should a colonial question his plans? "The route has been decided," he said. "Let it stand."

Troops began road-making north from Fort Cumberland.

Washington soon felt that he was in a nightmare, repeating over and over what he had done before. He knew the dangers and the grumblings, the disputes over grades, fords, passes, and rocks—all incredible to men who had never seen such mountains. But they went on, building.

In July the monotony was broken by two letters, one going, one arriving. Washington learned that a messenger was leaving for the south so he wrote a letter to Martha from camp. In part it said:

". . . Since that happy hour when we made our pledge to each other my thoughts have been continually going to you as to my other self. That an All-Powerful Providence may keep us both in safety is the prayer of your ever faithful and affectionate friend.

G. Washington."

Washington was not given to expressing himself about religion. But he had a deep sense of an all-directing God who

held the universe in his hand. He usually spoke of God as Providence or Destiny in the formal language of his time.

The other letter came by messenger from Frederick County. George hurried to meet the man when he saw him arrive; he hoped for a letter. Before they left for the road building he had announced himself as a candidate for the office of burgess from that county. He had meant to go to the election, according to the custom for candidates, but could not get leave. Had he lost the election because he was in service? He could hardly wait to open the letter.

"D'r. Burgess" it began—he was elected! The writing danced before his eyes; he steadied his hand and read on. He had led the poll. At twenty-six he was in the assembly. It was a proud moment. But of course he could not take his place there until this war was won.

Weeks went by. In October the weather was unseasonably bad. November began. Forbes was taken very ill but he drove the men on.

Many soldiers had signed on only until December; everyone had thought the war would be over long before then. Now officers wondered whether they could possibly reach the fort by the first. They pushed the work every daylight hour.

One night in late November, scouts took three prisoners. Washington turned them over to the proper officers for questioning. Perhaps now they would get some information about forces at Duquesne. He stood in the shadow watching as the questioning was done.

"You have been in Fort Duquesne?"

"Just left there."

"You are a British subject. You know you shall be hung for joining the enemy?" The prisoner squirmed. "You can save yourself by giving us true information about the fort. But only the truth will serve you!"

"I will tell you." The prisoner then said that the force was weak. The Ohio Indians had left. Washington took the news to General Forbes.

"This is our last chance!" Forbes cried. He selected 2500 of his best men and divided them into three brigades. One was under Washington. They were to travel light, with supplies coming up behind, and hack out a road to the fort. As soon as the tools came, the work began.

They traveled six miles one day, seven another, five another. The 22nd of November came, the 23rd. It was only a week now until December. Many men would then be entitled to go home.

Washington was writing by a campfire one evening when a scout came to him saying he had seen smoke. Had the fort caught fire? Had the French retreated? Minutes later another scout ran in. The fort was burned. The French had gone.

The men could hardly wait till dawn when they could get at the brush. Feverishly they hacked through a dozen miles that day. Night was falling when they came upon the remains of the wrecked fort. Someone counted thirty chimneys; others dug out worthless guns, piles of twisted iron, scalping knives.

The French had taken the cannon down the river. On an island, Indians waited, ready to go with the English, who might feed them.

There would be no battle, no death, no glory. The English could take the smoking ruins, but the disgrace of Braddock's defeat would never be wiped out.

Five years before, almost to a day, George had stood on this point and thought it a good location for a fort. Now he named the place Fort Pitt in honor of the prime minister who had sent Forbes to America.

As he stood by the great river, watching the ruins, he knew that youth and a dream of personal glory was gone from his heart. He had longed for the honor of a brilliant victory that would make him forget two failures and all the drudgery.

"I am through with military life," he vowed. "I shall return to Virginia and be a planter and a burgess. That is enough." He went back to his duties and his men.

In the cold light of the next morning he saw that considerable work must be done before he could give up military life. The site of the fort must be guarded; General Forbes was very ill, and neither food nor pay was at hand for the soldiers.

Washington was puzzling over these problems when a messenger came for him. "The general wants to see you at once, Colonel."

George hurried to Forbes' tent.

"Events here must be made known to the governor and the council at the earliest possible moment," Forbes said. "You know our condition. You know the wilderness. How far is it to Williamsburg, anyway?"

"Four hundred miles or more, perhaps, by the new road," Washington answered. Forbes shook his head, discouraged.

"Such distances! Well, you can travel faster than anyone I have. Plan to leave at once."

"Yes, sir!" Washington did not hide his pleasure in this assignment.

But bad weather made the long journey even harder than he had expected. Horses broke down from hard going and scant food. George was ill when he got to Winchester and had to delay for rest. He stopped at Mount Vernon; his clothes were worn and soiled. He must replace them before he went to Williamsburg.

The sight of his home refreshed him. Jack had carried out his brother's plans and furniture George had ordered even before he was engaged to Martha had come from England. He checked the list: a mahogany bedstead with carved and fluted pillars and yellow silk and damask hangings; window curtains to match; six mahogany chairs; a dressing table with mirror and brass trimmings. Everything he had ordered was in place.

Traveling on, George rested again at Betty's. Then at Williamsburg he made his report and attended to military duties so that money should be started north at once. Food had already gone from Fort Cumberland. After that he resigned his commission.

Now, at last he and Martha could set their wedding day.

At high noon on the sixth of January, George Washington and Martha Custis were married. The rector of St. Peter's church read the service in Martha's home. Among the many guests were Governor Fauquier in a scarlet, gold-embroidered coat with bag-wig and sword; Speaker of the House Robinson, English army and navy officers, and other men of distinction, with their ladies, wearing handsome gowns.

The bride was elegant in a gown of heavy silver-threaded brocade. High-heeled, white satin slippers with diamond buckles peeked from below an embroidered satin petticoat, flounced with lace ruffles. Her necklace, earrings, and bracelets were pearls.

The bridegroom was handsomely dressed, too. His blue coat was lined with red silk and had silver buttons. His waistcoat was made of white embroidered satin. Shoe and knee buckles were gold, and he wore a dress sword. With his height, soldierly bearing, and good looks, he was a bridegroom worthy of a rich and beautiful bride.

The newlyweds stayed awhile at Martha's home on the Pamunkey. Then they went to Williamsburg for the opening of the legislature. Here George, for the first time, took his seat in the House of Burgesses. With his own lands and his wife's plantations and other wealth (now all his according to the law), he might have retired to a life of ease. Many thought he had earned it. But he was interested in the colony and in public affairs. He looked forward to a busy life managing his plantations and serving the colony as a civilian.

Washington, Gentleman Farmer

The Washingtons went to Williamsburg at the end of January. Six Chimneys, Martha's town house, was ready to receive them. Word of their arrival got around before the coach was driven to the stable, and Mrs. Robinson put on her mantle and promptly came to call.

"Martha! I hoped you would come today!" the lady cried as she tripped across the room to greet Mrs. Washington. "The governor's weekly concert of chamber music is this evening—at the palace!"

"Tonight! But my hair!" Martha raised her hands to her brown curls in dismay. "Such a drive as we had down here—jolting all the way! The colonel was so kind." She looked at her husband proudly. "He rode in the coach with me all the way though he travels much faster on his horse!

"But tonight!" She remembered the concert. She pulled a bell cord and a houseman appeared at the door. "Send a messenger to my hair dresser at once. Tell him I need his attendance immediately."

"La, you'll never get that hair dresser today, Martha." Mrs. Robinson was amused. "His time has been engaged for weeks. The concerts are every Thursday."

"That is for him to manage," Martha said casually. "And tell Callie to start the sad-irons heating. I shall wear the blue satin and it will need a press." She waved the man away.

While the ladies chattered, Washington stood by the fireplace, entertained by this feminine talk. His "Patsy" fascinated him. She was so small, so meek and wifely, yet in her own way as strong as iron.

"The burgesses are arriving for the new session." Mrs. Robinson included him in the talk. "The season will be gay. Everyone—town people as well as the college—adores Governor Fauquier. You'll see, Colonel. Half a dozen of our best families sent their sons here to William and Mary College this year instead of to England. And so many young men are reading law with Mr. Wythe that Mrs. Wythe can hardly get a chance to have the library swept. And Martha, *did* you hear about Ellen's new London gowns?"

"I think I must leave you now, ladies," Washington said. "I have several matters needing attention."

A servant held his greatcoat, for the weather was still chill. Washington strolled to the Duke of Gloucester Street. Across to his left was Bruton Church, deserted this weekday. A half mile or more further was the handsome college building set in full view at the end of the street.

To his right was the capitol, at the opposite end of the mile-long street. Nearer was Raleigh Tavern where hitchracks were crowded with restless horses. Washington crossed over and entered the tavern; he would find friends there.

The governor's concert was delightful, as Mrs. Robinson had promised, but the bride and groom got more attention than the music. Martha looked charming; the hairdresser had "managed" for his wealthiest customer. Washington, of course, was the most distinguished military man in Virginia—the hero of three campaigns, as well as a man of wealth.

The next evening the Washingtons attended a play, an English adaptation of one of Molière's, and Saturday evening Speaker Robinson and his lady gave a dinner.

The town was pretty even in winter. White frame houses and larger dwellings of rosy brick were set behind white fences and borders of fragrant box. Parkways were green all the year; soon gardens, set between sycamores and great paper mulberry trees, would be gay with snapdragons, sweet Williams, pansies, and flowering shrubs.

On Sunday morning elegant coaches brought the Washingtons and many others to Bruton Church. Modest parishioners stood in the yard and watched arrivals with pride rather than envy. If everyone were rich and great where would be the fun of looking?

A few days later Washington went to the capitol on a new mission. This time he was no messenger, sent on a journey to the wilderness headquarters of the French. He was no commander begging food, clothing, and pay for his men. He was a duly elected burgess taking his place among men of growing power in Virginia. No man there had done so much; but his manner was so modest that few guessed his pride as he took his seat. Indeed his modesty was almost his undoing a few days later.

One of the members made a motion; it was recorded in the Journal of the House: "Resolved that the thanks of this House be given to *George Washington* Esq.; a member of this House, late colonel of the First Virginia Regiment, for his faithful Services to His Majesty and this Colony and for his brave and steady Behavior, from the first encroachments and Hostilities of the *French* and their *Indians* to his resignation after the happy Reduction of Fort Duquesne. . . ." That was in the formal record.

But one of the burgesses had a bit to add when he told the story that was repeated over and over in the town.

"Mr. Washington was called upon to stand," he said. "And there he stood by his bench, flushing redder and redder as the resolution was read. You know George."

Listeners grinned. They knew, too, that George was not an easy talker.

"When Mr. Speaker paused, George opened his mouth to reply—and I assure you, Gentlemen, not one word came from his lips! Robinson was quick to save the day.

" 'Sit down, Mr. Washington,' he said, smiling. 'Your modesty is equal to your valor and that surpasses the power of any language.' It was quite an occasion, I tell you!"

Washington was appointed a member of the Committee on Propositions and Grievances. The work of the house of

Martha was elegant in a bridal gown of heavy silver-threaded brocade. George's blue coat was lined with red silk and had silver buttons.

burgesses was done through committees; citizens asked for what they wanted or complained about what they did not get. The committee on which Washington served sifted all petitions, so he plunged at once into important government work.

The task suited Washington. He worked best in small groups where a man could speak his mind. Many letters were from soldiers; such were given him to act upon and he soon was known as the soldier's burgess.

His twenty-seventh birthday came when he was beginning to feel adjusted to his new work. If George remembered the inventory he had made at twenty-one, he might have been pleased now, six years later. The new burgess was tall and handsome, and had a dignity that made him quickly noticed.

Washington now had three residences—Mount Vernon, Martha's plantation home on the Pamunkey, and Six Chimneys. He had bought little land during his service, only 500 near Mount Vernon. Martha had brought him about 15,000 acres.

But his greatest assets were not material. He had a family —a wife and two charming children. From the moment he first saw them, George liked Jacky and Patsy Custis; he enjoyed the thought of them in his enlarged and hospitable home.

As for himself, Washington had learned to carry responsibility. He got along well with men under him; perhaps less well with superiors—partly because he lacked a sense of humor. Some thought that he was acquisitive and overly ambitious, but he was willing to work hard for what he got. His experience in military matters was unsurpassed by any contemporary.

Indeed, no young man in Virginia could match his attainments —probably no man in the thirteen colonies equalled him at twenty-seven years of age.

And now that he had resigned his commission and turned to civil activities, he meant to do his best—in the assembly and as a planter. When the assembly ended, the Washington family drove north to Mount Vernon.

Spring on the Potomac was a beautiful season. Lilacs and locust trees scented the air; fringe trees, dogwood, redbud, and fruit trees made a succession of bloom. Box borders were sweet, especially after a soft April rain, and perennials popped up with gay blossoms. Fields were brown and fresh from the plow; then bright green with new growth.

With Jacky clutching one hand and little Patsy perched on a broad shoulder, Washington showed his new family the home he loved: the west garden one day, the river the next. They saw the cook house, the carpenter shop, and the smithy, the barn and two new calves, and the stables.

The bride pleased her husband by proving to be an excellent housewife. At Williamsburg she was a social butterfly, but in her home she attended to spinning, weaving, preserving, salting meats, and baking. A Dr. Laurie was hired for fifteen pounds a year to look after the health of the people, but minor illness was Martha's business.

Mrs. Washington was a skilled hostess, too. Visitors came and found the mansion so pleasant that they stayed on.

In a few weeks Washington's days followed a routine that

he continued for years. After an early breakfast of tea and corn cakes he rode over his farms; there were five on the plantation. He used rail fences, called worm fences in Virginia, and these needed frequent inspections; he planned plowing, sowing, and harvests.

After a morning of riding, Washington came to the house for dinner in the early afternoon, usually with several guests.

"I like to eat plainly myself," he had told Martha, "but plan a bountiful table for our guests. If you need dishes, silver, or linens we will order from London by the next ship."

So a menu included chickens, duck and fish in season, ham, vegetables and fruits, and a variety of hot breads and preserves. For the late supper the cook made Brunswick Stew or some other hot one-piece dish. Fragrant myrtleberry candles, made at home, gave the light. Martha liked them better than whale-oil lamps. There was a feeling of leisure and comfort at Mount Vernon, very welcome after wilderness living.

But there was plenty of work, too, and need for alertness. One spring morning Washington and his overseer were inspecting near the creek when they heard a gun fired.

"That must be the poacher I warned off yesterday," the overseer said. The master of Mount Vernon did not reply. He whirled his horse, crashed through the bushes in time to see a poacher push into Little Hunting Creek.

"Be off with you!" Washington shouted in a temper.

The poacher lifted his musket impudently and shot another bird. Washington, flushed and angry, flung himself off his horse, splashed into the water, grabbed the boat and dragged it to shore.

"Now be gone!" he cried, tossing the gun aside.

The frightened poacher caught the gun in mid-air, pushed off frantically and paddled away.

Days when the weather kept Washington indoors he did "paper work" and he started a diary again to have a "Record of how my time is spent." On January 1, 1760, he set down:

"Tuesday, 1, Visited my Plantations and received an Instance of Mr. French's great love of Money in disappointing me of some Pork because the price had risen to 22/6 after he had engaged to let me have it at 20/. . . . found Mrs. Washington broke out with the meazles."

Wooden mold plows were used; Washington had an idea for a better kind. He wrote of his experiments in March:

"Fitted a two-Eyed Plow Instead of a Duck Bill Plow and with much difficulty made my Chariot wheel horses plow." Few would risk carriage horses in the field but Washington was impatient to make the test. Later he worked at his trees:

"Grafted 40 Cherrys. . . 12 Magnum Bonum Plums. . . Planted 4 Nuts of Mediterranean Pine . . ."

A year after the Washingtons settled so comfortably at Mount Vernon, Bryan Fairfax, George William's half brother, moved to Fairfax county. Lord Fairfax came from Greenway Court for a rare visit and the neighborhood was in a flutter of parties. Mount Vernon servants bustled about for days, laundering and polishing, stewing and baking for the dinner the

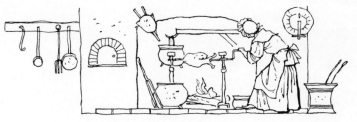

Washingtons gave for the newcomers. The Fairfaxes, George William and Sally, the Bryan Fairfaxes, and his lordship were there, of course, with the Greens, the Carlyles, and others.

After the ladies went into the drawing room to gossip, the men remained at the table to talk land and crops.

"I shall like living in Fairfax County," Bryan was saying, "but I hope I can get a living out of the soil."

"That's a problem we all face," Washington told him. "I have started keeping records to guide me. Last year my tobacco crop dropped to thirty-four thousand pounds."

"Are you sure, George?" Mr. Green exclaimed.

George nodded. "I'm growing some wheat. The trouble is harvesting it, a job that has to be done on the day the grain is ripe. One man cannot do more than three or four acres, either. But it makes a good crop. I mill it myself and ship it to Porto Rico."

"George grows other crops, too," Mr. Martin told Bryan. "He is putting in corn and barley and oats, I know."

"I thought I would plant some clover and rye," George said. "Last year I sent for books on agriculture in England, though their problem is different there. According to the books, land is dear and labor cheap." The men laughed.

"Not much like here," Martin said. "Land plenty cheap and labor dear and you're lucky to get it!"

"Corn wears the soil, though not like tobacco," George went on. "I plan to plant a different crop each year—have the records started now. And I shall try Lucerne (later called alfalfa). I have read that it is a good crop to plow under. I'm trying manure mixtures, too. We shall have to enrich our soil if we make the living you expect, neighbor."

A bell tinkled and the men heard Mrs. Washington's voice. "Bring fresh logs, Jed," she told the houseman. "The gentlemen will be joining us."

Washington grinned. "I think our business is finished, gentlemen?" he said, and they went into the drawing room.

Some days brought dangers. One stormy evening the creek flooded, and a slave ran to the mansion with the news.

"The mill dam is about to break, sir!" he cried.

"Call all hands to save the mill!" Washington shouted. He pulled on his boots and flung his great coat around him. The warning bell was ringing as he dashed out to run with the man. They were barely in time. The break in the dam was close to the mill; the whole building might be swept away.

"Fetch wheelbarrows!" he shouted above the roar of rain and rushing waters. "Get more shovels! I'll take yours, man!"

Washington took that shovel in his big strong hands and led the men in the work. In an hour the breach in the dam was checked; in two hours, he saw that the mill was safe. When he went back to the house, Martha and Jacky were at the door.

"You are soaked!" Martha exclaimed in distress. "Jed, take the colonel's boots and coat. Jacky wouldn't go to bed till you came," she added, and looked fondly at the tall man and small boy.

"I wanted to help at the mill!" Jacky complained.

"Tomorrow I shall ride over there to check the damage," Washington said. "If you were up and ready—"

"I could go with you?" Jacky cried, eyes dancing. "I'll go right to bed now, Mother." He climbed the stairs willingly.

In the morning Washington set the boy in front of him as he rode to inspect the damage. Their talk on that ride led the colonel to start Jacky's riding lessons, and as soon as it seemed safe he surprised Jacky by giving him a small horse.

"What shall I name him?" Jacky asked.

"That is for you to say," Washington answered. "We have Ajax and Magnolia, Valiant, and Blueskin—"

"Yes, I know," Jacky said. "Did you have a horse when you where a little boy?"

The colonel's eyes were thoughtful. "Yes, I had a chestnut horse, much like this one. I called him Whitefoot."

"Then this one is Whitefoot, too," Jacky said.

Then, so that little Patsy would not feel neglected, Washington sent off an order to England. She was to have gloves, toys, bonnets and "1 fashionable dressed baby doll."

Happy family life and the task of getting the plantations in shape were engrossing. After some four years, Washington began to look about for more land. He heard of vast swamp areas in southeastern Virginia, known as the Dismal Swamp, and thought possibly those might be drained and made useful.

At the end of the session of the assembly in the spring of 1763, he rode to the swamps, and went again in the fall, when

he made a careful inspection and wrote a report. With five others, he organized a company for draining and using that land. A good deal of money was spent, but all that resulted in Washington's lifetime was the production of some cypress shingles.

About this same time, Washington was elected vestryman for Truro Parish, where his father had served. Usually this honor was given before a man was elected a burgess, but Washington's long war service reversed the order. He served the parish for twelve years and the assembly for fifteen.

The organization of local government in Virginia made a kind of school for leadership. A planter must learn to manage his own place: the people, crops, marketing, and shipping. A vestryman had a wider responsibility for roads and local justice, as well as civil, church, and welfare business.

Membership in the house of burgesses was the next step up. Burgesses managed a good deal of the colony business. This gradual training provided Virginia with experienced leaders who were ready to serve the larger colonial community when they were needed.

In much this way, years passed happily at Mount Vernon. They were busy, prosperous years. Washington's war service was all but forgotten; people thought of him as a family man —a country gentleman. He seemed to have everything that an ambitious man could want.

But all the while, under the placid surface, fate was stirring, a fate that would call him again to service.

Rising Unrest

"Mount Vernon never looked more beautiful," Washington remarked to Martha on a sunny May day in 1763. Turning from the view over the Potomac he picked up a copy of the Gazette that a messenger had just delivered, and glanced at it.

"Well! At last England and France have signed the peace treaty," he exclaimed.

"Peace *now!*" Martha was astonished. "I thought that war was over before we were married."

"Oh, the fighting, yes. But it always takes men a long time to fix up a peace." Washington smiled at her as he went toward the library. "Please have Jed order my horse. I shall ride over and discuss the news with Fairfax, my dear."

As he read, Washington found disturbing news in his paper. Pontiac, that brilliant Indian chief, was fighting the British; the news made a man uneasy. But Pontiac and Detroit were far away, Washington reminded himself. And he had retired.

The Indian revolt made the English realize that they must protect their colonies. That would cost money, and they were

Years passed happily at Mount Vernon. Washington's war service was all but forgotten; people thought of him as a family man—a country gentleman.

already in debt from the war just ended. Defense money should come from the colonies, parliament said, and laid a tax on imports of molasses. And by 1764 colonial ports were closed to all but English ships so that the British could have all profits from trade.

Northern colonists were more annoyed than southerners; indeed their feelings for England had always been different. Pilgrims came to the new world to get away from religious persecution, Puritans to escape a dictatorial government. Time had tempered their emotions; now trade restrictions awakened old prejudices.

Southern colonists, especially Virginians, had close ties with England dating from the days when younger sons left home to make fortunes in the new world. England was spoken of as "home" even by native Virginians. A duty on molasses did not, at first, strain ties of long standing.

But duties on molasses did not bring enough money. The new prime minister, George Grenville, needed more, so in 1764 he planned a "Stamp Tax." This would require that government stamps be put on newspapers and all legal papers, bonds, insurance policies, and deeds. The money raised was to be for colonial defense, but that did not make colonists like Grenville's method of raising it.

A storm of protest rose, in the colonies and among Englishmen who did business in America. Benjamin Franklin, in London, spoke brave words against the Stamp Act. Boston held a town meeting to protest. James Otis, an advanced thinker about colonial rights, published a paper against it that was circulated throughout the colonies. Soon angry letters were on their way to London. Washington wrote many himself.

"The Stamp Act engrosses conversation (he wrote in a letter to a relative of Martha). What may be the result. . . I will not undertake to determine. . . The eyes of our people already begin to be opened." He said that the act would fail.

The Stamp Act came up for discussion in the Virginia assembly soon after a new member, Patrick Henry, had taken his seat. Henry was gifted with a fiery eloquence rare in the Virginia assembly. When the Stamp Act was being discussed he rose and boldly declared that only the Virginia assembly had the right to tax Virginia citizens.

"Whoever says otherwise is an enemy!" he shouted.

"That is inflammatory talk," Speaker Robinson retorted.

"My statement is justified by the nature of the case, sir," Henry said. He went on to talk of colonial rights and as he was closing his address, he said, in his eloquent best:

"Caesar had his Brutus; Charles the First, his Cromwell; and George the Third. . ."

"Treason! Treason!" A dozen men sprang up, shouting.

". . . may profit by their example," Henry finished smoothly, quite undaunted. Then he turned to the corner whence the loudest shouts had come. "And if this be treason, make the most of it!"

But in spite of protests, the Stamp Act passed in 1765.

Colonists did not accept it meekly. Massachusetts called

a conference for October in New York. The act was to take effect in November. Nine colonies sent delegates who made formal protest to London. Virginia, and three other colonies who did not attend, sent similar letters. None was heeded.

George Mercer, Washington's army friend, had been appointed in charge of stamps for Virginia. He came to Williamsburg and publicly declined to serve. People shouted approval.

"Down with the Stamp Act!" men cried.

"Good for Mercer! We're for you, George!"

"Have a parade! Let's show him!"

Boys gathered wood and built great bonfires along Duke of Gloucester Street. At twilight bells rang, fires flamed and shouting men marched down the street. Women crowded the walks and children ran alongside, abreast of their fathers.

Boston and New York had parades, too. Feeling was so intense that loyalists had to watch their words.

England soon began to feel a difference in her relations with the colonies. Benjamin Franklin was questioned about it.

"The colonies have had not only respect but affection for Great Britain; for its law, its customs and manners and even a fondness for its fashions. . ." Then he paused.

"And what is the temper now?" he was asked.

"Oh, very much altered," he said quickly. "I doubt if the Stamp Act can be enforced."

Franklin was right; the act was repealed the next year. But the colonies never resumed their former relations with England.

Resentment took several forms. In Boston bickering grew worse when the governor refused to allow James Otis to take his elected place as speaker of the assembly. Massachusetts resented trade restrictions and the effort to make all colonial governments alike. Troubles led to bloodshed in the Boston Massacre in 1770.

No blood was shed in Virginia, but the assembly took a firm stand and voted that they alone had the right to tax Virginians. Moreover, they sent copies of this document to all other colonies. Then they applied to the king—ignoring parliament—for relief from the wrongs they suffered.

Lord Botetourt, the new governor, was shocked; he dissolved the assembly. But that did not bother the burgesses. They marched down Duke of Gloucester Street and reconvened in Raleigh Tavern. There George Washington presented a bill that he and George Mason had written. It pledged that Virginians would buy no English merchandise that was taxed by parliament.

This bill was named the "Non-Importation Agreement" and it passed immediately. Copies were sent to other colonies in the hope that this boycott would be shared by all.

"My family will take this hard," a burgess remarked soberly, after the vote was announced. "My wife gets her gowns and bonnets from London. But she will obey it."

"I have a big order of furnishings for our new house ready to send," another said. "I wonder what I could buy in the colony?"

"My neighbor has a craftsman who makes good chairs," a man answered. "If you have a pattern to show him, he might help you out."

Word of skilled cobblers, clockmakers, pewter craftsmen and such passed from man to man and colonial crafts were rapidly improved. This was a happy and unforeseen result.

The frontier, a factor in all the troubles, was still uneasy in 1770, when Washington decided that he must journey west and see about lands promised soldiers years before. He went to Alexandria and talked with his good friend, Dr. Craik.

"I get letters from soldiers who never received their land pay," he said. "The area has not even been surveyed. I was to have five thousand acres myself—I do not know where. How would you like to go out with me and look the region over? We would go beyond where we served with Braddock."

"How far?" Dr. Craik wondered.

"To Fort Pitt first; that is familiar to us. Then by canoe down the Ohio. That would be adventure." Washington was enjoying the idea.

"Would we make our own camp?" Craik asked.

"Yes. We would take two or three servants. We are not boys any more, James! They would help carry food and guns; we would hunt game when we could."

"You are daft, George! But I shall go with you!"

They were twelve days getting to Fort Pitt, then they went down the Ohio to the Great Kanawha. The soldiers' land was located around there. They selected plots, made surveys, and went on as far as the Muskingum, and back for more surveys at the Kanawha.

When he reached home, Washington began writing letters to soldiers about their land. Strobo and Van Braam were in England; George bought their land and sent the money to them. That was the only way they could collect that back pay.

This same year, 1770, concern for Martha's children put a damper on the gaiety at Mount Vernon. Jacky had continual trouble with his tutors and Patsy was seriously ill. Washington took her to Warm Spring; the baths did not help her. He had several of the best doctors, but in spite of all they could do, Patsy died in June of 1773. Martha's heart was heavy for a long time.

It was in this year, perhaps as a help in diverting his wife, that Washington began making plans for enlarging and beautifying his home. He expected to add to the house, build new buildings around it and improve the gardens and grounds. The first step would be to build additions on each side of the present house, each the full height of the present two and one-half stories. He sent to England for needed materials.

In 1769 Washington had built a house in Alexandria. The town had grown to be the third largest seaport in America; new warehouses, shipyards, and rope factories lined the river's edge. It was an important place for shipping and other business. Washington often stayed there for several days at a time; Martha, too, came to shop and to visit.

After a while the Washingtons seemed to feel a tenseness

among their friends as frictions increased. Many Scots lived in Alexandria; the Fairfaxes were loyal to the king. The words "Whig," meaning colonists who rebelled against parliament, and "Tory," those who remained loyal, began to be used though many people did not take a stand either way.

Feeling between Whigs and Tories was more intense in Massachusetts where Samuel Adams was the leader of the Whigs. In 1772 he had called a town meeting and created a "Committee of Correspondence" to exchange views and information with other towns.

In Virginia, life went along quietly. Governor Botetourt died, and the Earl of Dunmore came to take his place. Dunmore called the assembly in March of 1773 to smooth out the disputes with parliament. To his amazement, the burgesses set up a Committee of Correspondence—like Massachusetts. Only they went further. Letters were to be exchanged between colonies, not only towns, about all matters "relating to the common good." This interchange of letters was the first successful effort to unite the colonies.

Dunmore saw that the new committee was dangerous. He dismissed the assembly and did not recall it for one year. It reassembled in time to hear that the port of Boston had been closed. In protest, the burgesses ordered a day of fasting and prayer. A page carried the news to the governor.

"They *dare* not!" Dunmore shouted. "They insult the king!"

"Dare not?" The burgesses were angry when they heard

that. "Are we Virginians—or cowards?" They stormed out when Dunmore dissolved the assembly.

"We've met in Raleigh Tavern before," one burgess cried. "We seem to be getting the habit." The men marched down the street and reconvened. They made the fast day official and ordered their committee of correspondence to call for a congress of delegates from all the colonies.

Bruton Parish Church and other churches in the colony were packed on the first day of June. And during June and July county meetings were held throughout Virginia. Washington was chairman of the Fairfax county meeting at Alexandria and he was ordered to write a letter of protest to the king.

This letter was to list grievances: unfair taxes, sudden dismissal of the assembly, the taking away of a colonist's right of trial by jury and other disputed matters. The letter said that the colonists had the right of self-government—but it also expressed loyalty to the king. It begged him not to reduce "his faithful subjects in America to desperation, and to reflect that from our sovereign there can be but one appeal." This threat of rebellion was approved by Washington.

The county meetings elected delegates to a Virginia convention to take the place of the dissolved assembly. It met in Williamsburg in August, 1774. Washington presented the Fairfax county letter and then spoke for it.

"This, I assure you," he said, "is the true feeling of the people I represent." He closed with a promise: "I will raise one thousand men and march to the relief of Boston."

After that the convention appointed seven delegates to the First Continental Congress, planned for September in Philadelphia. Washington and Patrick Henry were delegates. Washington gave ninety pounds toward travel costs to make sure all could go.

When the congress opened, all colonies but Georgia were represented. Of course there were many shades of opinion among delegates. Massachusetts men, remembering the "Tea Party" only three months earlier, were for independence; Virginia was with them. To others the very word "independence" was appalling and disloyal. One delegate mildly proposed a union of colonies with a president appointed by the king—George III would never consent to that!

The congress worked for fifty-one days. Then it accepted a set of "Resolves and Resolutions" which were sent to the king, the British nation and all the colonies. It adjourned to meet the next year if all grievances were not righted by that time.

Since the meetings had been secret, people were curious about what was going on. Someone asked Patrick Henry who was the greatest man attending.

"If you mean eloquence," he answered thoughtfully, "I say Rutledge of South Carolina. But if you mean solid information and sound judgment, Colonel Washington is the greatest man on the floor." Many were of that opinion as the congress disbanded.

Shops in the big city were enticing. Before Washington

left for home he bought a pocketbook for Martha and a cloak for his mother.

But to Martha's dismay, he could not take up his former happy routine at Mount Vernon. He had public duties. Small independent companies of militia were organizing in Virginia, and many sent for the colonel to come and advise them. Massachusetts wrote for his advice. He received hundreds of letters, all to be read and answered. Farming and fences must wait.

A year passed. In March of 1775 the Second Virginia Convention opened in St. John's Church in Richmond, Virginia. There Patrick Henry spoke in favor of arming Virginia militia. At the close, he said eloquent words that stirred listeners:

"Gentlemen may cry 'Peace! Peace!' but there is no peace. The war is actually begun! The next gale that sweeps from the north will bring to our ears the clash of resounding arms. Our brethren are already in the field. Why stand we here idle? Is life so dear or peace so sweet as to be purchased at the price of chains and slavery? Forbid it, Almighty God! I know not what course others may take, but, as for me, give me liberty or give me death!"

For seconds men sat in stunned silence. Then they rose, shouting arguments. The resolution for arming was passed by a close vote—but it did pass.

Events followed fast after that. In April the governor moved Virginia's ammunition from the powder house in Williamsburg to a ship. At that, Patrick Henry led a protesting, shouting crowd to the palace. The governor had to pay Virginia for what he had taken. He declared Henry an outlaw, but Patrick represented Virginia at the next congress, just the same.

That same April, the British general, Gage, who had been keeping the port of Boston closed, decided to seize some stores in Concord. Watchful Whigs warned the countryside to be ready. A lantern in a tower and Paul Revere in a midnight ride aroused Minutemen who took a stand on the green at Lexington. The British came; they fired a single shot—then a volley. In an hour the place was swarming with Minutemen. The British retreated, pressed by the Minutemen who began the siege of Boston.

These stirring scenes in Virginia and Massachusetts were happening at the very moment when delegates left home for the Second Continental Congress to open May 10, in Philadelphia. In stage coaches, at inns, people spoke their minds to the delegates.

"Are you planning to talk while the British shoot?"

"You men better *do* something!" was repeated over and over.

Delegate Washington evidently had action in mind; he came to the congress in military uniform. He had not worn it for sixteen years but it fitted him perfectly. Buttons shone; it looked like new. His appearance seemed to say: "War is coming! I am ready."

People stared at him on the street.

"Who is that tall military gentleman?" many asked.

"That's Colonel Washington. He served in the war with the French—remember?" those who knew answered with pride.

In the meeting, his imposing figure, air of distinction, and military readiness set him off dramatically against the others in ordinary blue and brown business suits.

As work of the congress got underway, Washington was put on several important committees—to plan finances, provide ammunition, raise an army. Maryland and Virginia pledged to march to aid Massachusetts, the colony in the most dire need. Perhaps other colonies would join, too. If so, there should be a leader to co-ordinate efforts. Who should that be?

A Marylander nominated George Washington to be commander in chief; his election was unanimous. The next morning, when he was formally notified, Washington thanked the Congress for their trust and added, "I do not wish to profit from the government. . . I will keep an exact account of my expenses . . . that is all I desire." He foresaw that army service would cause him financial loss; an owner must be on the job if a plantation was to make money. But he did not hesitate.

June 15, 1775 was the date of his election. Five days later he was handed his commission as commander in chief of the colonial forces for the defense of American liberty.

George Washington was now forty-three years old. He had been a soldier; he was a vestryman, a burgess, a planter. Until this day, no one seems to have thought of him as a leader of the people. Perhaps until this momentous moment, the people had not needed the kind of leader he was to become.

The Continental Army

News of the battle of Bunker Hill came to General Washington while he was traveling north from Philadelphia. It made him ride even faster to join his command.

John Adams had proposed a name for this militia—"The Continental Army"—and Congress had approved. The name was to show the king that rebel colonists were not against him; their quarrel was with the British ministers. To emphasize that point, British forces in America were called "The Ministerial Army."

"The Continental Army" must have seemed a high-sounding title for the forces the general saw in Cambridge, Massachusetts, on the second day of that July. Hundreds of colonists, fired by angry enthusiasm, had rushed to enlist. The greater number, naturally, were from Massachusetts; but all colonies were represented.

"Parliament has no right to stop trade!" men cried.

"We didn't dump tea!" New Yorkers shouted angrily. "Parliament should let us alone."

Those who had muskets shouldered them, those who had none went along, hopefully; and all gathered at Cambridge.

But after the battle of Bunker Hill, where colonists fought bravely and lost for lack of powder, the mood changed. Many decided they had enlisted hastily and returned home.

Washington took formal command on July third, 1775, in a simple ceremony on the village green. Then he inspected the camp. It had a shabby, hodgepodge appearance; shelters were made of sailcloth or boards, stone and turf, or brick and brush. Cooking arrangements were bad and there was not enough food. Men wore their own jeans and hunting shirts.

And all the while, across the river on Boston Neck, British soldiers were well clothed, fed, and housed in a comfortable camp. Moreover, they had guns, cannon, and ammunition. The colonists had skill and courage—they had killed twice as many as they lost on Bunker Hill—but they had little else.

Soldiers eyed the general critically as he inspected their lines. He held his spirited dappled-gray to a slow pace and looked right and left, deliberately.

"You kin tell he means to be boss," a Vermonter remarked thoughtfully—after the general was out of hearing.

"This place is in bad shape, Jake," another man said. "Maybe a boss is what we need."

Down the line a tired South Carolinian straightened his spine when the general looked his way.

"I sorter like a general who looks like a general," he told his buddy later. "That Washington is a Virginian—but I like him anyway. I'm goin' to shave."

A Massachusetts man had meant to slip off home that

night. He was hungry for green-apple pie. But he changed his mind.

"Let's not go tonight, Josiah," he said. "Let's give the general a chanct to show what he kin do."

Washington inspected and studied and then began to remake the army. The task was the more difficult because the enemy might strike any moment. Colonists did not know that General Howe would not risk another bloody Bunker Hill, that he chose, instead, to sit in camp and wait.

Colonial equipment was bad enough but Washington soon found that morale was worse. Soldiers blamed the Continental Congress for all the shortages—cannon, muskets, powder, food, and clothing. Hundreds had brought their own firearms; two thousand had none. At one time they had only nine rounds of ammunition—with the enemy in sight across the Charles River.

One morning as the general made his early daily inspection he had the feeling that he had come upon a quarrel.

"What have we here, Lieutenant?" he paused to question a young officer. The man gulped. Dare he speak out?

"The men are a bit put out, sir," the lieutenant looked straight into Washington's steely blue eyes. "A new captain has taken over. He is from Virginia. We're New Yorkers."

The general's lips twitched and his eyes grew friendly. "With a Virginian in high command that would seem too much," he said, and the young officer paled. "I am making needed changes. Report to me at four this afternoon."

The lieutenant and others met that afternoon in the general's office. A map lay on the table—carefully drawn, like a surveyor's map. The camp was to be divided into six brigades of six regiments each. Men were grouped by colonies and as far as possible under officers from their own colony.

"We have no prospect of uniforms, gentlemen," Washington told the group when the organization had been explained. "But you will be given bits of ribbon. Wear these in token of your rank. This will help the men recognize their officers. I have purchased a piece of blue ribbon to distinguish myself." The aides wore green ribbon; majors and brigadier generals, pink. One order of the day announced: "No soldier is to appear on parade with dirty face or hands or uncomb'd hair on pain of being punish'd for disobedience of orders."

But in spite of all efforts at improvement, men went home. Often the general did not know how many were in camp. But those who stayed grew steadily stronger in skill and morale.

At the end of each busy day Washington wrote countless letters; his pen raced over the paper with messages to governors, Congress, and influential men. His task was threefold: watch the enemy, train an army, and wangle supplies. He needed authority, a sense of justice, friendliness, knowledge, and firmness. He used all this—and sometimes even his hot temper.

Camp gossips spread one tale of temper that boosted the general's reputation. Two soldiers, one from Virginia, the other from Massachusetts, had a quarrel that grew into a fight. An orderly dashed to report to the general.

"Sir!" he cried, "they are having a fight—over there!"

Washington rose so quickly that a chair overturned, and his papers fluttered. Speechless, he rushed outside, sprang onto his horse, whirled, and was off. Leaping a fence, he galloped across lots in the direction the orderly had pointed.

"The general's a-coming!" a youth yelled.

The crowd fell away. A glance at Washington's stern, angry face sent them scurrying—all but the two fighters, locked in each other's arms.

The general leaned from his horse, grasped the fighters, one in each powerful hand and shook them until their teeth rattled. Then he dropped them, gathered up the reins and without one word, rode back to headquarters.

However, all matters were not so promptly settled. The continental position back of Boston prevented the British from getting supplies by land. But they had a good navy; they were still well fed. Washington obtained the help of fishermen and put soldiers aboard their little boats. These stopped British ships and the steady flow of supplies. That did worry the British. It also worried the townspeople in Boston.

"Suppose that rabble army should take a notion to attack our city!" they asked each other anxiously. "We'd be ruined." But since Howe did nothing, Bostonians, too, must wait.

In the late autumn a terrible epidemic of smallpox climaxed Continental Army misfortunes. Thousands sickened; morale dropped to a new low. Washington was rewarded for the pain and mortification he had suffered in Barbados, years before. He went freely about the camp to make sure the sick had care.

"Ain't the general feared of catching it?" a sick man asked.

"He's had it," another said. "When he was twenty."

"But he's *handsome!*" Half a dozen men, covered with ugly sores, looked toward their general.

"Ay, and he married a rich and pretty woman. A man from Virginia told me," a lieutenant remarked.

"Then I reckon we kin make out," a Vermonter said.

Because of the epidemic, Washington stayed on at the camp. In June, when he came north directly from Philadelphia, he had expected certainly to go home for the winter. Now he could not leave, nor could he ask Martha to come and visit him.

But Martha thought more of her George than of danger. She arrived, prepared for a long visit. The general was happy —but worried, too. He wrote to England for information about Dr. Jenner's new idea of vaccination. The answer said that this treatment appeared to protect some; others became very ill; some died. He decided not to mention the treatment to Martha. But he told her not to come near the camp.

No one ever thought of Martha as heroic, she was such a small gay person. But when she realized that George was so concerned, she bravely "took the pox" as inoculation was then called. She was ill for a few days, and then recovered safely.

After the new year, two events, neither of them military, sparked the public thinking. Thomas Paine wrote a pamphlet called "Common Sense." In it he urged colonists to strike boldly for freedom from England, for liberty, and for happiness as an independent republic. Thousands of copies were circulated in the colonies. People read it and talked about it everywhere.

The idea of independence from England startled Washington. He had hoped for a peaceful settlement of disputes—no more. But Paine's ideas were logical, he thought; maybe they were right.

Then there was a flag. Earlier, Washington and Franklin had been on a committee to choose a flag that would be a symbol of the colonies' joint efforts in the Continental Congress and in the army. A design with thirteen alternating red and white stripes with the Union Jack on blue in a corner was chosen. Washington assembled the troops and made a ceremony when it was raised over the camp in January, 1776. Men had various thoughts as it fluttered on top of the flag pole.

"A bit of cloth!" Some were scornful. "We need powder!"

"A new flag," others thought, "and this camp of men from many colonies is new, too." They were puzzled to find themselves deeply stirred.

But even with a pamphlet and a flag the army still needed guns and powder. Henry Knox, one of Washington's officers, was a Boston bookseller turned soldier. He wanted to do something about the lack of arms, so he went to the general.

"Come in, Colonel," Washington had become friendly with Knox; he trusted this man. "I hear you have a plan?"

"I have, General," Knox answered. "That is, if I am rightly informed that some cannon are idle at Ticonderoga?"

"That is correct," Washington said. "I am told they have

been there since the fort was taken. They are too far west to do us any good, alas!"

"I volunteer to fetch them, sir," Knox said. "I can get men to go with me."

"But have you thought—" Washington looked closely at Knox and saw determination in his bearing. "I am glad to give permission and may fortune be with you, Colonel!"

Knox and his men dragged fifty cannon and some other supplies on forty-two crude ox-drawn sledges over frozen lakes and snowy hills. The welcome the camp gave them must have warmed even their frosted toes!

Now, secretly, the Continental Army began to fortify Dorchester Hill, high ground overlooking the British camp. The men worked at night, digging trenches and hauling cannon into position. Hard work was a relief after weeks of inaction.

On the morning of March the fourth, General Howe looked up at cannon, trenches, and soldiers. He was astonished.

"We shall attack immediately," he ordered.

But at that hour, nature took a hand. A terrible storm of sleet, snow, and wind prevented attack. When the storm passed, the opportunity was gone. Washington's army was so strongly fortified that they could easily destroy the British.

In a parley, Howe agreed to leave Boston. He promised not to burn the city behind him, if his men were allowed to leave.

This made a dilemma for General Washington. He, too,

could destroy the city. If he let the British leave—and saved
Boston—would they really go to Halifax as Howe promised?
Or would they go to New York or the Carolinas?

Washington held council with his staff and they favored
saving the city. So on the seventeenth of March, the British
troops and many Tory townspeople, loyal to the king, left
Boston. As the general watched the frigates load he must have
thought of another victory without glory: the taking of the
smoking ruins of Fort Duquesne. As on that day, no blood
was shed in this victory. He left for New York very soon to
take charge there.

Martha packed up to follow him and then go on to Mount
Vernon. But before she left, she talked with Billy Lee, a trusted
servant Washington had brought with him.

"You take good care of the general, Billy," she said. "See
that he eats right and doesn't work all night."

"Yes, ma'am," Billy replied. "That is, ma'am, I'll try."

Mrs. Washington smiled. She had not been able to stop
the night letter-writing. What could Billy do but try?

After the letters on army business were written, Washington often wrote to his overseer at Mount Vernon. For this post
he had chosen a distant relative, Lund Washington. He wrote
Lund his plans for crops, fences, and stock, and about the additions to the house. Lund marveled that a man could keep so
many ideas in his head. It was hard enough for Lund to reply
two or three times a month! One of Washington's letters said:

". . . Let the hospitality of the house, with respect to the

poor, be kept up. Let no one go away hungry." He explained to Lund that he had no salary for war duty and added: "It becomes necessary . . . for me to be saving at home."

In New York, Washington heard more and more talk about "independence." In May, Virginia ordered its delegates to propose independence. In June, Richard Henry Lee spoke for Virginia in the Continental Congress and said, "These united colonies . . . ought to be independent." The word was on hundreds of tongues.

Congress had to take heed. They appointed a committee to state clearly the ideas of the people. Printed words would give all the chance to read and to understand. Thomas Jefferson, Benjamin Franklin, and John Adams were among the members of that committee.

Jefferson was known to be a good writer and he had thought deeply about the needs of the people. So the committee asked him to write out what he thought such a paper should say. His words were read at the next meeting. Men thought he had done well, but they made some changes. They wanted each word exactly right.

The document first listed the causes of friction with Britain. Then it stated clearly three tenets of the proposed new government: all men are created with equal rights to life, liberty, and the pursuit of happiness; governments are formed to get these rights for all people; Britain did not give Americans such rights, so Americans proposed to make a new nation, the United States of America.

The paper was read in Congress on July second. Cheers greeted the approval of this Declaration of Independence.

After the formal acceptance on the fourth of July messengers on fast horses carried the news and the copy to be printed. People waited eagerly and grabbed moist sheets. As they read the words of the Declaration many understood for the first time what the quarrels and the fighting meant. Until that moment many had been fighting for their rights as Englishmen. Now they saw they had a larger cause—freedom for all men in a new nation.

Washington was on Long Island preparing to defend New York City when copies of the Declaration of Independence were brought to him. That evening, July 9th, he ordered the army drawn up in companies and had the declaration read to each group by "men with good voices."

On the Sound, British frigates were crowded at anchor. Staten Island was covered with a huge British camp. Any hour might bring a battle with the odds against victory for those listening men.

Erect on his horse, Washington listened with the others. The bold words rang out clearly on the evening air. Emotion surged like a flame through the ranks of ragged men; the eloquent words carried a new hope to their hearts. *All men are created equal.* Here was an ideal for which a man might be willing to give his life.

Fighting for a Cause

The words of the Declaration were thrilling but all too soon Washington and his army on Long Island were confronted by hard military facts. General Howe had gone from Boston to Halifax; but he had stayed there only long enough to gather supplies and recruits. He arrived on Staten Island in July. By August he had 32,000 well-equipped men in camp there, and was supported by British frigates in New York Harbor.

Washington knew that the port of New York was a vital asset. Since spring he had been strengthening its defenses. Now, in midsummer, the city at the tip of Manhattan Island was fortified; water approaches were guarded and to the north Fort Lee and Fort Washington seemed adequate. Twenty thousand soldiers manned these fortifications. A ridge on the western end of Long Island was fortified, too, and 7,000 men guarded this eastern approach to the city.

It was here, on Long Island, that General Howe attacked. For three days the United States army fought bravely against overwhelming numbers. Washington saw the terrible casualties, yet dared not bring reinforcements from the city lest the British attack there, too. But he must save his army.

At twilight he rounded up as many barges as could be found and began moving his army to Manhattan. All night, the general stood by, watching as each barge loaded and was pushed off, returned and reloaded. At daybreak a thick curtain of fog allowed the last man and cannon with the commander himself to make the crossing to New York City.

That successful night-ferrying of thousands of men has been called one of the great military feats of history. But it was bitter humiliation to the army of the newly united states.

British troops next entered the city. They forced Washington north; they took the fort bearing his name. They pushed him onto the mainland; they took White Plains.

The commander called his staff for conference.

"We are not equipped for battle against these forces," he confessed to them sadly. "If we fight and lose—the whole cause of independence will be lost with us."

"If we could only keep the army together," a lieutenant began.

"Could we not harrass them, General?"

"Yes, you voice my own thoughts," the general agreed. "Keep our army intact. But for harrassing action we need shelter back of us. I propose that we cross the Hudson to open country where we have freedom to move—and a forest behind us. The British do not know how to fight in a forest."

"But general," someone asked anxiously, "suppose the British should push on to Philadelphia? What then?"

Sleepy Hessians grabbed muskets and rushed out. Washington threw himself on a horse and rallied his men to pursue the Hessians down the street.

"We shall retreat beyond the Susquehanna River," the general said quickly. "To the Alleghenies if necessary. But we shall *keep our army!*" His eyes glinted. "As long as we have an army in the field, England must keep an army here to fight us. Even the wealthiest nation cannot continue that expense for a long time." The staff heartily approved his words.

So they crossed the Hudson. In that autumn of 1776, the British had Long Island, Staten Island, and Manhattan. Tories who had been forced to move out of New York came back and settled in comfort. The British held Rhode Island and parts of New York and New Jersey, and seemed about to take Pennsylvania. A frightened Congress hastily moved from Philadelphia to Baltimore for safety.

Americans were confused and disheartened. General Howe offered security to all who would sign an oath of allegiance to the king. People balanced a dream of freedom against promised safety—and thousands signed. Thousands more, who could not bring themselves to sign, feared that the cause of independence was doomed.

In fright and despair Congress turned the war over to Washington with full power to act.

The general knew that a dramatic victory would renew faith and inspire men to enlist, so he made a bold plan. He had learned that three regiments of hired Hessians and a troop of English Light Horse were in Trenton, New Jersey. His soldiers hated those Hessians—men hired to fight against liberty! They would welcome the chance to attack them.

The town of Trenton was spread along a street at right angles to the Delaware River. In comfortable homes, which did not belong to them, Hessian soldiers ate and drank by blazing fires, and began to celebrate Christmas.

Across the river in the early darkness of Christmas night, 1776, Washington and twenty-four hundred devoted soldiers crept to the river. There they had hidden twenty cannon and some boats—not enough, but all they could find.

"We divide here," the general whispered directions. "You to the left," his motions could hardly be seen in the black darkness. "You to the right, as planned. I shall keep with the center section. Be across, ready to march promptly, at midnight."

Floating ice floes delayed the crossing. The general peered into the blackness—were the others across? He did not know. It was four in the morning when his own boat crunched against the icy bank; there was no time to search.

General Greene was to take half of Washington's party, march inland, and come upon the village at the far end of the street. Washington and his half were to advance near the river.

"I count on you, General," Washington whispered, and both sections set out. Rain turned to sleet and glazed snow that reached men's knees. If there was a path, they never found it. Panting, they plodded on.

Washington's party arrived at the town first. He deployed his men around houses near the river and when all were in position, gave the signal, *"Fire!"*

The spatter of bullets wakened the Hessians as the sound

of Greene's muskets echoed from the other end of town.

Sleepy Hessians grabbed muskets and rushed out. Americans fell back behind trees, bushes, house corners, and reloaded. Washington saw a horse hitched under a shed. He threw himself on it and rallied his men to pursue Hessians down the street. There Greene's men captured them. Nearly a thousand prisoners were taken in a fraction of an hour.

Other Hessians and troopers slipped off between houses. Washington wanted to follow them; if his other sections had come, the town would have been surrounded. But he must think of the prisoners they already had, and the weather. He recrossed the river. That was the surest way to hold his gains.

There, opposite Trenton, they made camp. Soon the other sections joined them. Across the river the British quickly gathered reinforcements to attack. This time, they felt sure, they would completely crush the rebels.

Washington, too, was convinced that the British force was strong, so he chose strategy instead of attack.

"Have the supplies of wood doubled," he told an aide. "We need great fires tonight." That seemed natural enough in the bitter cold. But when the fires blazed, whispered orders sent the men away, through the woods. The British sentinels watching the camp fires did not suspect that the enemy had vanished into the darkness.

In the morning, Washington and his men were miles away. They made their second surprise attack and took the village of Princeton. After this Howe did not dare to stay in New Jersey.

He withdrew his army to the safety of New York.

These victories were relatively small and local, but they proved inspiring. Men enlisted, proud to serve under a brilliant general in the cause of freedom. On this cheering note, Washington and his army went into winter quarters at Morristown, New Jersey, and Congress returned to Philadelphia.

Now that Washington was successful, many people were sorry they had signed the oath of allegiance to the king. The oath was no protection, they found; British and Hessian soldiers stole and destroyed without asking who was friend or foe.

General Washington thought the time had come to make his own proclamation. He announced that people who had signed Howe's paper and had now changed opinions could turn in those papers and take a new oath of allegiance to the United States of America. He allowed thirty days, so that any who wished to live where they could be British subjects could move.

Some people, especially some congressmen, criticized Washington for this. They said loyalty was the business of the various states, that new government machinery was not ready.

But Washington was sure he was right. He boldly risked his reputation and his future and insisted that people must declare their allegiance or move away. He won his point.

As the winter passed, the need for secrecy about the size of the army and lack of supplies became embarrassing. Washington dared not let his weakness be known; yet the public, believing that the army was strong, expected him to do more than was possible.

"Better be blamed for weak leadership," he told General Greene, "than risk the cause by attempting too much." Greene thought Washington was right.

Martha came to Morristown for a visit that winter. She had learned to knit and her fingers were busy making socks for soldiers as she sat by George and his inkstand. He wrote countless letters about the exchange of prisoners, enlistments, supplies, and late at night—about his plans for Mount Vernon.

Spring came; summer days grew hot and still there was no victorious battle. Washington wondered whether Howe was planning to attack Philadelphia. Or would he move to the Hudson and try to divide the states? Perhaps he would march to New England? With only about four thousand regulars Washington could not take the offensive.

Late in July the general went to Philadelphia for a conference. Coming from that meeting he chanced to see a young man in the hall.

"I don't recall seeing him before," Washington said.

"You haven't, General," said a congressman who was with him. "That is the Marquis de la Fayette; he has just arrived from France. I hear he is an idealist and a friend of our Dr. Franklin. When he read our Declaration of Independence he was so fired with zeal for our cause that he left his country, his wife, and his home to join with us. Congress has given him a commission as major general—an honorary rank of course. He insists on serving without pay."

"I wonder—" Washington watched the youth's brisk gait.

"I wonder if an honorary rank will satisfy that young man. His bearing cries for action!"

"But, General," the congressman protested, "Lafayette is only nineteen!" Washington laughed.

"The Marquis reminds me of myself at nineteen," he said, "eager for glorious action."

That evening Washington attended a state dinner where he met Lafayette. The warm affection which he had felt at first sight grew as they chatted across the table. "This is a youth I would like to have had as my son," Washington thought. A longing for the son and heir he never had made him take the handsome Frenchman to his heart. As they left the table Washington drew Lafayette aside.

"We welcome you to our country," he said warmly. "You show a noble spirit, thus coming to our aid." The young man's eyes glowed with frank hero-worship.

"It is nothing, sir," Lafayette answered in excellent English. "I shall feel well repaid if I can serve under you."

"That would please me," the general said. "Meanwhile, when you can, come to my home at headquarters. I shall count you as one of my family."

"You are kind, sir!" Lafayette flushed with pleasure.

"Wait and see," Washington warned, a twinkle in his eyes. "We have no luxuries, no conveniences. But what we have, you may share."

Soon after this dinner party, it was learned that Howe had a fleet in Chesapeake Bay and planned to attack Philadelphia. Congress was horrified. Members promptly forgot a scheming intrigue to make General Gates commander in chief. They passed a resolution of confidence in Washington and begged him to protect them. Their real hope lay in him.

Washington saw that the people as well as Congress needed confidence. So he planned a great parade to stir patriotic pride.

"But, General!" His aides were shocked with their orders. "A parade requires uniforms, shining muskets, marching skill —we have nothing to make citizens proud."

"We have a cause," the general reminded them. "We have loyal soldiers. And we shall do our best.

"The men are to clean the clothes they have," he ordered. "Every musket must shine. Since men have no common insignia, have each wear a sprig of fresh green in his hat."

The camp was lively with activity; men made new verses to old songs and sang as they did their washing and shampooing. Fife and drum corps practiced "Yankee Doodle" and men joined in:

> "The bell that rang at Lexington
>   Had called our men to arms;
> And but their wives and children, now,
>   Remained to work the farms."

Faithful Billy Lee listened as he pressed Washington's uniform and polished buttons. He felt sympathy for the men. The majority of the soldiers had left farms—as Washington had. The new republic was an agricultural nation.

The August day of that parade was hot and clear. Breakfast was out of the way early and men fell in line promptly.

"March by fours!" the order came. "Leave space between each line! Fife and drum corps march in the center of each regiment." This made the line seem long and impressive.

The commander in chief led the parade and never had he looked more assured and handsome. At his side rode Lafayette,

representing the French co-operation. The gold on his major's uniform was dazzling in the sunshine. The parade wound through the one-time Quaker village, now the richest city in the new world. People went wild with pride and new hope.

But a brave front was not enough when the small army faced the larger British forces at Brandywine and at Germantown a few weeks later. The British won both battles.

Congress demanded an explanation, and Washington reported that a rainstorm had ruined ammunition. Before more arrived the enemy slipped away. And "why I did not follow immediately . . . (he wrote) . . . is the lack of shoes. At least a thousand men are barefoot. . ." His fury leaped from that paper—an army without shoes!

This was the autumn when Gates, Washington's rival, defeated the British under Burgoyne in the north, pushing Washington's popularity down to a new low point.

Trees dropped their leaves of red and gold; icy winds blew. The army under Washington must have winter quarters. A section of wooded land northwest of Philadelphia was chosen. It was named for an old iron furnace on Valley Creek Road which the enemy had destroyed in September—Valley Forge.

Valley Forge to Yorktown

The location at Valley Forge gave the army fine natural defenses. Mount Joy, the highest hill, overlooked the countryside for miles around. On a clear day the watch could actually see Philadelphia, where the British relaxed in comfort and plenty. Lower hills and ridges were well adapted for fortifications. These hills were exposed to bitter winds, but they were fairly safe from attack.

Washington appointed Brigadier General Louis du Portail, an engineer of the French Army, in charge of building defenses. Du Portail was one of several competent military men who came to the aid of the new republic. Baron de Kalb of Germany and Count Pulaski of Poland were at Valley Forge, too.

General Knox had charge of artillery. He and his men brought forty-two cannon to Valley Forge and set them up in the hills. The colonists had turned the old forge into a munitions factory, but the British had burned that. So Knox built a log shop where his mechanics repaired old weapons and made some new ones.

Planning the housing for the soldiers was a task Washington kept for himself. He designed a small, snug log hut, with a fireplace, to house twelve men. Each hut had a stick-and-mud chimney and six bunks on each side wall. Hospital huts and shops were planned, too, and the whole camp was laid out.

Some companies were sent on ahead as soon as the plan was made. They cut down trees—eighty thousand in all—and began building. By the time the camp was finished, the woodlands had vanished, but the soldiers were sheltered from wind and snow.

Only a few huts were ready when the first companies dragged themselves into winter quarters on the nineteenth of December, 1777. The men were in a frightful state from hunger, cold, and illness. It had taken them a week to travel fifteen miles to the new camp; their bare feet left a trail of blood on the snow. Hut-builders made great brush fires and the exhausted men lay, feet to the flames, until huts were finished.

The plight of the United States Army in the lush Pennsylvania countryside was tragic. Farmers refused the money their congress issued. A slang phrase, "Not worth a continental!" showed the public's opinion of paper dollars. Congress, that year, was a loosely organized group of delegates—ambassadors, in a way—from the states. They had no power to levy taxes; they could only beg the states to give money. All the while, the British had plenty of gold and bought all they wanted. But the American soldiers at Valley Forge were hungry to the point of starvation.

Washington spent the daylight hours inspecting, planning; at night he wrote letters ordering, even begging, for supplies.

"Where is the general living?" a soldier asked.

"In a tent," his sergeant answered. "I heard that he told General Greene he would stay there until all the men had shelter. Then he'd find a place for headquarters."

Later Washington moved into a small stone house near the Schuylkill River and the camp took on a more settled routine.

The camp was planned by states, an idea that worked fairly well at Cambridge. A year and a half had passed since the Declaration of Independence was made but the words "American" and "United States" were only slowly coming into use. Men at Valley Forge seldom thought of themselves as Americans or as in the United States Army; they were still Vermonters, or Virginians. They liked to be with their neighbors.

After their meager supper, the dozen men in a hut sat around the fire and talked.

"What you figure we are here for?" a gaunt man from Massachusetts asked his buddies.

"We're fighting for freedom!" a thin-faced soldier answered.

"Freedom! A lot of good this freedom does me! Don't make me laugh. M'belly's so empty it rattles," the gaunt man cried.

"I'm serious," the other man said. "Didn't you read that Declaration? Once this is over we'll all have a better chance at living. The general says so. I trust him—don't you?"

The men were silent and thoughtful. Most of them did trust the general. Those who did not, deserted.

Military custom allowed no direct contact between a general and a private soldier. But as they saw their general riding hither and yon, day after bitter cold day, they felt a pride in him; a warm respect for a cause he believed was worth such sacrifice. For he, too, might be at home, in comfort, had he chosen.

At twilight, when storms abated, men built brush fires and gathered around to sing. Washington did not sing, but he loved music. Often he stood near, listening with pleasure. Singing made the camp seem a happier place.

Those early weeks at Valley Forge drew men together. The sufferings and the rare moments of joy created a bond that men felt deeply. Other winters would bring miseries perhaps even worse; other seasons, new troubles. But this time, this place was unique in the nation's history. Through the years since that December of 1777, the words "Valley Forge" have come to be a symbol for man's steadfast devotion to a cause.

And so the winter wore on. Martha heard rumors of hardships, but she arrived for a visit in time to celebrate George's birthday, his forty-sixth. Word got around camp and groups celebrated the best they could. This was the first time that the general's birthday was observed outside of the Washington family.

On a day in March the sun shone brightly and the first hint of green showed through streaks of melted snow. Washington, inspecting camp, saw a group of men playing ball on a level bit of ground. He dismounted and handed the bridle to an aide. Memories of games he had played at Austin's home by Pope's Creek stirred pleasantly in his mind. This, he saw, was some new game, not merely tossing ball.

As he strolled near, a ball came swiftly toward him. The general reached out, caught it, and pitched it back.

The crowd yelled approval. When they saw that it was the general who had caught that fly, they cheered again.

"What is this they play?" Washington asked a captain.

"It's a new game to me, General," the captain said. "They call it 'Rounders.' The four stumps that make a square are called 'bases.' One man pitches. A batter hits and a man tries to run around the bases before the ball is caught."

"Want to pitch, General?" The shout came from a bold Virginian at second base.

Washington tossed his coat to the captain and pitched an inning. After that Rounders was a feature of camp days. Men whittled bats from barrel staves; others made balls of bullets wound with yarn from the top of a ragged sock and covered with a bit of cloth. Men from South Carolina played New Yorkers while crowds, often including the general, watched them.

At headquarters life was a bit more comfortable after Mrs. Washington came. Food was poor and scanty. But Martha set the table with a few treasures she brought from home, lit myrtleberry candles, and supper became a party. For dessert there were nuts, which Washington enjoyed. While other men smoked, he cracked nuts between his strong thumb and fingers, and they talked about the country's business and future.

During the day, Mrs. Washington worked for the men. She invited officers' wives to her room to sew for the soldiers; Mrs. Knox, Mrs. Greene, and others knitted and patched during the mornings. Afternoons they visited the sick. A daily sight at camp was small Martha in a great shawl and snug bonnet, tripping alongside a tall sergeant who carried a covered bowl of steaming soup that she had made. Hours were as full for her as for the general.

One day, a stout florid foreigner came to Valley Forge and asked to see the commander. After some delay and much difficulty because of his German tongue, he was admitted.

"I have a letter from your Franklin," he said, bowing low.

Washington did not understand the words but he took the letter and began to read it.

"You are Baron Frederick William von Steuben?" He glanced up at the stranger, who bowed again.

"Ja!" he said. "I wish to offer my service to you, sir."

Washington read that in Franklin's letter, and also that the baron was an expert on military tactics. An aide was sent to fetch interpreters, and soon half a dozen men were sitting by a fire in the general's front room.

"We welcome you, sir," someone exclaimed heartily.

"You are the very man we need," another said. "We have men and a cause. But we lack the skill to create a disciplined army."

"We are not a military people," an officer explained. "We are farmers, booksellers, teachers, blacksmiths, and carpenters.

We do not know how to go about making a real army."

The next day the baron inspected the troops gathered on a meadow under Knox's guns. The sight shocked him. The soldiers were thin and hollow-eyed; many literally had not enough clothing to cover themselves. How they must love their cause, he thought, to remain faithful to it under such hardships.

Von Steuben began the training at once, starting with a hundred men who would then become teachers of others. Their ineptness and independence alternately astonished and angered him. His quick temper flared, and his rages were frightening. One day he exploded into a torrent of swearing—and suddenly realized that the men did not understand a word that he was saying!

"Come!" he shouted in German to an aide. "Swear for me in English!"

Flushing hotly the young officer spoke a few words. Someone laughed. The baron whirled, frowning. Then he laughed, too; he roared till his fat sides shook. Laughter rippled over the drill field and saved the day. The peppery baron kept the men drilling for weeks, till they became a creditable militia.

As these weeks passed, some frictions developed between men under hardships and in close quarters. There was a plot against Washington; many wanted Gates as commander in chief. When Lafayette came to Valley Forge, some on the staff were jealous of the affection between the commander and the Frenchman. Under the long stress, more soldiers deserted;

when caught, they were severely punished. That made resentment—and more discipline.

But even more disturbing than camp frictions and jealousies
was the ever-present worry about the British army. Why didn't
Howe attack? He knew the plight of the patriots at Valley
Forge. Spies gave him plans of the fortifications and news of
shortages. Did he hope to wear out American patience? If so,
he knew little of Washington and his training in the wilderness, years before! But Howe did not attack; Washington
never knew why. Instead, Howe made a gesture of peace.

Spring was spreading warmth; dogwood blooms and songbirds were on the Pennsylvania hills when the peace offer came.
Four years earlier the colonists might have accepted the terms.
But since then, they had declared their independence. They
relished their freedom even though they did not like war. The
peace offer was refused.

After that, changes came among the British. Howe resigned, and Sir Henry Clinton came to take his place. Clinton
had a new idea on how to win the war; he proposed to defeat
one state at a time. As a first move he left Philadelphia, moving his army and quantities of supplies to New York.

Washington was stirred to quick action. How glorious if
he could take that great train of men and baggage! He followed with his now well-trained army and forced the British
to fight at Monmouth on the 28th of July. He had half promised Lafayette that he could lead the charge but at the last
minute General Charles Lee insisted that the honor was his.

But Lee, instead of meeting the British directly, angled away. Washington rode so furiously to rally his men that a favorite horse fell dead under him. The general quickly mounted another and went on. He was able to check the British but not to defeat them. In the night they slipped away.

After this disappointment the war settled into a three-year doldrums with only minor fighting. New names, new battle areas were in the news. George Rogers Clark took Vincennes; John Paul Jones sailed the seas; Cornwallis, under Clinton, attacked in the south. Indians terrorized Pennsylvania.

Outfitting men and ships was expensive; the new republic was hard-pressed to find money. Robert Morris and Haym Salomon impoverished themselves to help. Betty Washington's husband, Fielding Lewis, turned his iron works into a munitions plant and lost his fortune. Many patriots gave everything for the cause of freedom and the young nation lived because of their sacrifices. Looking back, later, men wondered how they had endured.

A climax came at the end of 1780. Soldiers in miserable winter quarters at Morristown were hungry, poorly housed and clothed—and had had no pay for months. When they heard that new recruits were getting twenty-five dollars in "hard money" for enlisting, they mutinied. There was a riot and bloodshed.

"I'm going to Philadelphia and get my rights!" a soldier yelled, and hundreds more took up his cry.

Fortunately word came to Washington at once. He under-

stood his men; they wanted only the rights that they deserved. He worked out a compromise and the mutiny ended. But the general wondered how long he could keep his army that way.

Cornwallis continued to ravage the south. Many Americans believed that the British would give up the north, take Florida and the Carolinas and make a separate nation. Washington did not agree. He held on at West Point and kept British troops near there watching him. He sent some of his best generals and forces to the south where Cornwallis was attacking.

In March, General Greene won a victory of a sort at Guilford Courthouse, North Carolina, and Cornwallis headed toward Yorktown, Virginia, where the British navy could rescue him if necessary. Greene followed him while Washington, still hoping for more French help, watched every move.

A French ship came to Newport with word that Admiral Count de Grasse would sail from the West Indies in the summer. Washington replied that with the French commander Rochambeau they could attack either New York or Yorktown. Which did de Grasse prefer? The admiral chose Yorktown.

Washington gave up his dream of taking New York and made new plans. He left part of his army to guard the north and, joining Rochambeau, headed south. By the time they reached Yorktown, de Grasse had beaten off British ships and was in position across Chesapeake Bay. Cornwallis could not escape.

Excitedly, French and American troops dug trenches and

set up batteries of cannon forming a V, one side French, one American. On the afternoon of October ninth, the French fired the first shot in the attack. Two hours later, Washington himself lit a fuse that set off the American cannonade.

The terrible bombardment lasted for days; it riddled the British defenses and the little town nearby. Washington was ever in the midst of the battle; one day he dismounted, handed the bridle to a sergeant and joined General Lincoln and General Greene at a battery. The risk of a British shot worried his aide.

"This situation is very exposed, sir," he ventured.

"If you think so," the commander said, "you are at liberty to step back." Neither man moved. Soon a shot did strike close by. General Greene took Washington's arm and pulled him back as the ball rolled at their feet.

"We can't spare you yet, General," he exclaimed.

"It is only a spent ball," Washington answered.

On the nineteenth a white flag fluttered above a British redoubt and a drummer beat a call to parley. Firing stopped while surrender terms were sent to Washington. He refused these, but later his own terms were met. Cornwallis had no choice.

On the day of formal surrender, dogwood flamed against golden maples and copper beeches and oaks. Beyond the battlements the wide York River flowed peacefully and in the distance the bay sparkled in the sunshine. French ships-of-the-line were spread like stepping stones from cape to cape.

The victors were drawn up in a mile-long line: the French at one side, headed by Rochambeau; the Americans on the other with Washington. The British marched between them, their colors furled. British General O'Hara brought word that Cornwallis was ill. Washington, mindful of his country's honor, turned to his own second in command.

"It is for you, General Lincoln," he said. Lincoln accepted the sword and then returned it in a generous gesture to a brave officer. All the British were allowed to keep their sidearms and personal property.

The great victory, the glorious day, the music of army bands and fife and drum corps stirred loyal hearts. Few remembered that the war was not yet ended. But from that hour, no one, not even the British, doubted which nation would win.

A Man of Many Interests

Relays of fast horses carried news of the York-town victory to Congress, nearly 300 miles away. When the messenger burst shouting into the hall, the delegates went wild with joy and relief. Cheering, they voted thanks to General Washington and, as a gift, two stands of colors captured from the British. They next voted gifts of ordnance to Count de Rochambeau and to Count de Grasse, and funds for a marble column to be built at Yorktown. No one was heard to mention that generous support earlier would have been more effective.

The news of victory stirred the country. People stood in the streets, reading newspapers. They hailed each other joyfully.

"Cornwallis is taken!"

"We've won the war!"

Only the Tories were silent. These loyal British subjects in America were dismayed at the unexpected turn of events.

Washington well knew that the war was not won; the British still held New York and Charleston. But with help at once, he could strike a final decisive blow. A message to Count de Grasse asked if he would stand by in New York harbor;

the army would go there promptly. The admiral declined. Another message asked the admiral to stand by at Charleston, on his way south. The answer was again no. De Grasse had an appointment in the West Indies.

The commander himself carried his third idea to the flagship. He made a call of ceremony that had a double purpose: to thank Admiral de Grasse for aid in trapping Cornwallis and to persuade him to convey two thousand troops to Charleston on his way to the Caribbean. Graciously—but firmly—the admiral declined. Landings might be troublesome; his agreement with Spain required speed.

A feeling of frustration overwhelmed Washington as he returned to his headquarters. The strenuous days of the siege of Yorktown, the stirring battle, the glorious victory—was it all for nothing? Was the war to drag on? Well, he could only continue with the resources he had.

General Greene, in the south, needed help. Washington sent some troops to him and started others on the long march north. British prisoners must be housed and fed until they could be exchanged. Countless details were decided.

A page of the general's diary, much neglected during the war, lay open on his desk. He was writing notes when the sound of galloping hoofs made him pause, pen above the paper.

"Lieutenant Custis is dying!" a haggard rider panted.

Washington ran out, threw himself onto a horse and galloped off. That half-finished sentence in his diary was an eloquent record of his shock. He reached Eltham, the home of

Jacky's aunt, as Jacky Custis died. The young man, only twenty-eight, had been serving as an aide on the general's staff when he was taken ill. Mrs. Washington and Jacky's wife, Eleanor, were numb with grief. Fortunately the general had finished his more pressing tasks and could go with them to Mount Vernon.

Death had now taken both of Martha's children from the beautiful home where children were loved and wanted. Jacky's young widow was left with four little ones; the youngest, named for the general, was only six months old. George and Martha adopted him and the youngest daughter, called Nelly. The two older girls went with their mother to her family home in Maryland. Later she remarried, but she continued the happy custom of visits to Mount Vernon.

The responsibility of planning for two young children was good for Martha in the hour of grief. The general followed her meekly around the house while she made decisions.

"This shall be Nelly's room," she said, choosing a west room on the second floor. "We must get a proper crib for her."

"And this will be for the baby." She decided on a small room next to the yellow bedroom. "It will be handy for us." She chose a nurse and fixed a daily routine for the babies.

About this time Lafayette felt he must return to France. Washington could hardly bear to part from him. The young man's idealism and good spirits had been a joy for more than four years. The general felt doubly bereft. But he, like Martha, found comfort in pressing work that must be done.

The war was at a stalemate. The British had been shocked by Cornwallis' defeat, but they still had New York. Patriots felt that the Yorktown victory had won the war. They wanted their men to return home. Washington knew that to make a good peace the army must continue successfully until actual papers were signed.

Plainly, a struggle with Congress was his next duty. He left Mount Vernon for Philadelphia.

From there he wrote to General Greene, in December, 1781, that he feared the states would send no more money for the army. He wrote that he was staying in Philadelphia ". . . to impress upon Congress and get them to impress upon the . . . States the necessity of the most vigorous exertions." Congress still had little power; it could only recommend and try to persuade the states.

Next Washington wrote to all the governors begging them to support the army even to the moment of negotiation for peace.

All that winter Washington remained in Philadelphia working with grafting contractors, fretting soldiers, indifferent Frenchmen, and a procrastinating Congress. The worst problem was money—currency. Congress printed money with nothing to back it. People cunningly paid debts with paper money that had trifling purchasing value. Washington himself had loaned money and suffered losses by repayment in paper money.

People in England were tired of the war, too. Britain had won most of the battles, but the few American victories were decisive: Trenton, Princeton, Saratoga, and Yorktown. British posts at Wilmington, Savannah, and Charlestown were gradually abandoned. Clinton awaited orders to leave New York. Steps toward peace began.

In April Washington had orders to cease hostilities and formal work on the treaty proceeded. On the third of September, 1783, in Paris, the peace treaty was signed recognizing the new nation, the United States of America. Two years after Yorktown, eight years and more after Lexington, the army celebrated victory.

But the commander knew that hard work lay ahead: the task of making thirteen states into one nation. He decided that he should express his thoughts on this subject to the governors. In a letter to them he wrote:

"This is a time of political probation . . . the moment to establish the national character forever." He admitted that civil matters were not a general's business but ". . . in the present crisis, silence in me would be a crime." Then he listed four points which if followed he believed would make a strong nation:

A union of states under a federal government.

A regard for public justice and honor in paying war debts.

An army for mutual defense.

A willingness among the people to forget prejudices, make concessions and sacrifice for the good of all.

That agreed on, a nation founded on liberty would grow to be a glorious country. He begged the governors to think over these words.

In October, 1783, Congress discharged those who had
served in the war, retaining only a small force until a peacetime militia was organized. So the day came, November second, when the general must bid his troops farewell.

Washington's eyes roved over the ranks of soldiers before
him. He had looked forward to this day, the end of war. Yet
now that the moment had come he could hardly speak. With
these men he had suffered cold and hunger, disappointment
and frustration. With them he had seen comrades shot down.
Where would he again find friends like these? His heart was
too full for speech; yet they looked to him, expectantly.

He spoke kind, fatherly words and begged them to care
for the Union they had helped create. He told of his friendship
for them and desire to serve them, always. He gave them his
blessing and ended . . . "the commander-in-chief is about to
retire from service. The curtain of separation will soon be
drawn and the military scene to him will be closed forever."

Tears rolled down the cheeks of these men who had been
hardened by suffering. Silent, they parted.

Soon the general went to New York to finish army business. The governor of New York gave a banquet for Washington, the French staff, and other notables. There was another
leave-taking when the general boarded a barge to cross the river
enroute to Annapolis. He waved his hat and called, "Good-
by! Good-by!"—a rare gesture for the reserved Washington.

Martha, looking very pretty in a brown silk dress, drove
to Annapolis to see the ceremony as her husband resigned his

commission. With a few other wives she sat in a balcony of the Maryland state house while the general walked forward and laid down his sword. Washington said a few words as he surrendered "the trust committed to me" and commended his country "to the protection of Almighty God."

The next morning the Washingtons, escorted by three young aides, left for Mount Vernon.

"You look happy, General," one of them remarked as the general climbed into the coach to ride with Martha.

Washington chuckled. "Why wouldn't I be? I got a load off my shoulders yesterday. Now I can enjoy my grandchildren."

Trunks strapped on top were packed with gifts for Jacky's four children who would be at Mount Vernon for Christmas.

Early twilight had come when the travelers reached the west door of the mansion. Lights glowed in the windows. Servants ran out, shouting greetings. Children rushed from the house in welcome. Joyously they clung to their grandfather and dragged him inside.

The house was gay with Christmas greens. Fragrance of myrtleberry candles, apple logs burning, and pine branches mingled with whiffs of savory food being hurried to the table.

The young aides could not get to their homes for Christmas, so Washington kept them at Mount Vernon to share the merriment with family and neighbors. As they were leaving a few days later he gave each one a gift of one hundred dollars for expenses on their journey.

When they were out of sight, Washington went to the barn. The smell of hay was delicious; the stomp of horses' hoofs welcome. He passed housemen carrying wood; from the house he heard little Nelly's reluctant music.

"You may stop practicing now, Nelly," Martha's voice called down, and the children scampered into the hall to greet their grandfather. This was home as he had dreamed of it for eight long years.

After the holidays Mount Vernon was snowed in by a storm; the general had time to take stock of himself. He was fifty-two now, and quite gray. His eyes had wearied, writing by the light of one candle. His teeth had suffered from bad army diet. He had had many colds and some malaria and rheumatism; but above all, he was tired.

Army habits were hard to break. Washington often wakened with a start. "Was that the call to reveille?" he would exclaim, only to find himself in his comfortable bed at home. He missed Knox and Greene and Robert Morris. He would have liked to talk with Anthony Wayne and "Light horse Harry" Lee and others. Mount Vernon was almost too quiet while the snow kept him indoors.

But as soon as the weather changed, planter Washington was out with Lund, inspecting, planning, working—happy again. Lund had done well, but the plantation should produce more. And there was the remodeling, begun but not completed. They would get at that as soon as the crops were in.

While traveling about, on war duties, Washington had

seen some fine estates and had talked with Frenchmen and Americans from other areas. As a result, he had new ideas about improving farming and beautifying his house.

"Around Morristown, farmers rotate wheat, barley, corn, clover, and peas," Washington told Lund.

"You have rotated crops before, General," Lund said.

"Yes, but not on such a scale. Nor with so little tobacco. I am numbering my fields and shall keep an accurate record of harvests so we shall have facts to guide us in the future."

As for changes in the mansion, Washington found that Lund had carried out directions very well. The south addition, a library with the general's room above it, was finished, and Lund had hung Lawrence's portrait in place of honor. The north addition was built but the interior was as yet incomplete. Lund had built the unique cupola and several outer buildings, called "dependencies," which replaced small old buildings around the mansion.

Now Washington finished the great pillared veranda on the river side; he ordered flagstones from England for the floor and acquired thirty Windsor chairs. These, he hoped, would invite relaxation in the cool shade.

Then he laid out a serpentine drive bordering a three-quarter mile green between the west gate and the great front door. Along with all this he began planting trees and shrubs. The estate was to be as beautiul as he could make it.

To Washington's surprise, work was continually interrupted by visitors. Noah Webster came to ask that the general

recommend a newly published spelling-book. Old soldiers and foreigners arrived. One Englishman was interested in what the general wore. His diary reports that mornings, while on farm work, Washington wore a "plain blue coat, white cassimer waistcoat and black breeches and boots." Indoors, he wore "hair neatly powdered, a clean shirt . . . drab coat, white waistcoat and white silk stockings."

Several painters and sculptors arrived to do commissions. Washington poked fun at himself and his sittings for painter Robert Pine. He wrote to a friend: "At first I was impatient . . . restive as a Colt is of the Saddle. The next time . . . less flouncing. Now no dray horses move more readily to the thill than I do to the Painter's Chair."

The state of Virginia had engaged sculptor Jean Houdon; he had come from France to model the general. But Washington could not picture himself in the Roman toga Houdon planned.

"Couldn't you make some little deviation in favor of modern costume?" he suggested tactfully.

Another interruption to the work on Mount Vernon was the quantity of mail. Washington received hundreds of letters from friends, soldiers, foreigners, crackpots, and beggars—endless letters! He had outside interests, too: Dismal Swamp, a plan for a canal between the Potomac and Ohio Rivers, Rumsey's invention called a steamboat, and the opening up of the west. Washington's mail piled high, and finally he engaged

Twilight had come when the travelers reached Mount Vernon. Servants ran out, shouting Christmas greetings, and the children clung to their grandfather.

a young man as a resident secretary to help him cope with it.

Most men of that day were thinking of their country as a strip along the Atlantic. But Washington thought of America as a great nation, extending westward. He decided to inspect his own lands along the Ohio and other properties. Dr. Craik, Bushrod Washington, brother Jack's son, and three servants took a journey of nearly seven hundred miles. They went in the autumn of 1784. Washington returned much refreshed by this outdoor life.

After that journey, life at Mount Vernon was gayer. The diaries tell that dogwood bloomed; that the fringe trees transplanted well; that cherry and pear trees were set out, too. Acorns and buckeyes which George brought from the Monongahela shores sprouted and grew; he went fox hunting; he and Martha danced at many a ball. . . .

The squire of Mount Vernon had come home.

A New Government Calls

The people of America rejoiced when the war was officially over. Like the Washingtons of Mount Vernon, they wanted to settle down and live as they had before the rebellion. One year passed, then two and three. People began to see that the United States of America had grown to be very different from the thirteen former colonies. Even though a family lived in the same house in the same town, life around them was changed.

On a bright spring day in the middle 1780's, a group of women lingered outside a church on a Sunday noon. Over the nation, it was a common thing for such groups to visit awhile. They gossiped and talked about these "modern" times.

"My husband can't get over how different everything is since he came home from the army," a friendly, middle-aged woman said. " 'You're always clanking your loom,' he says. But when I sell the cloth, the money is handy."

"Didn't you always sell cloth, Mrs. Weston?" a young married woman asked. "I've been knitting and selling socks and caps since I was ten!"

"You're too young to remember how it used to be, Susie," Mrs. Weston said. "Times began to change when they got that law they called a 'Non-Importation Act.' That stopped us buy-ing things in England."

"My folks never bought from England!" Susie exclaimed.

"No, nor mine either," a plump woman laughed. "But look what happened! My husband had a little cobbler shop; he made common shoes and did repairing. But it wasn't six months after that act till folks from fine houses came to him beg-ging him to make shoes. He used their old ones for patterns."

"And now he has a factory and ten men working for him," Susie said. "I never knew that he started that way!"

"Maybe you don't know how my husband started," an-other said, turning to the younger woman. "He liked to work with metal—made a pretty cup for Dick when he was a baby —my Dick who was a drummer boy in the army. My husband never thought of selling anything; we had a little farm near town. But twelve or fifteen years ago folks came asking would he make a candlestick or a plate. Now he has a big pewter business."

"Other farm folks had changes, too," a neatly-bonneted woman said. "Take my sister. Her husband went to war. No-body could keep that man from serving under General Wash-ington. But my sister and her five children had to eat. She learned to plow and plant and harvest; you couldn't hire a hand in war times. Now that he's home, Mary's so used to manag-ing that Ned's bought more land. When you get a woman started, it's hard to stop her."

They laughed and went home to cook dinner. All over

the country, similar changes had come about through the years.

People were changing their ideas about slavery, too. In the North, people earned a living on farms or in crafts and industries. Local people worked for wages; it did not pay to own slaves. Even in the South, where slaves were thought necessary on plantations, intelligent planters like George Washington began to wonder if slavery was a good idea. A slave had no future to dream of and work for, as the poorest of free men did. Freedom to work for himself made a difference to a man.

Many planters were troubled by the moral idea of holding slaves. The Declaration of Independence said that all men were created equal; what about slaves? But it was not clear just how to end the system; so most men, like Washington, did nothing. (But in his will, Washington freed his slaves.)

Underlying most problems was currency. Government bonds bought by patriots went down to ten cents on the dollar. Gold and silver money—British, French, or Spanish—was as valuable as ever. But paper money issued by Congress and by the various states would buy very little. Something must be done—but what?

The government of the United States had been trying to get along under rules adopted in 1781, the "Articles of Confederation." These helped at the beginnings; they were a "league of friendship" between the states "for common defense and general welfare." But now the Articles were not enough.

The new republic did not have mother England to appeal to. Of course it was good to be free, but free men must stand on their own feet. Spain was strong on the Mississippi, France in the north, and Britain in the northwest. Could the separate states protect the country? Many citizens were old enough to remember that colonies could not work together against France in the 1750's.

George Washington had foreseen this danger; that was why he had written that letter to the state governors before he retired from the army. He read with interest the opinions of one of his young friends of army days, Alexander Hamilton. As a youth, Hamilton had come to New York to attend King's College, later Columbia University. He had joined the patriot army in 1776 and become one of the commander-in-chief's aides. Washington read that Hamilton, and others, were working for a new agreement between the states to take the place of the weak Articles. Hamilton's ideas were not popular at the moment.

"Let our government alone," men said.

"Give us time! We'll make out!"

By 1786, the form of government for the new republic was argued on street corners and in taverns. Newspapers took sides. Food cooled at dinner tables while tempers grew hot. But talk helped the people to make up their minds.

A group of Virginians, urged on by James Madison, asked their legislature to call a convention of the states in September. The special purpose was to make uniform laws about navigation and shipping. Only five states sent delegates, but the leaders refused to be discouraged. They persuaded that little convention in Annapolis to ask the Congress to call a meeting of all the states in Philadelphia the next year.

For a wonder, Congress was willing. It called on the states to send delegates to a constitutional convention in May, 1787. All but Rhode Island responded. Now surely something would be done to get firm, responsible government.

A list of the men who came to that meeting was a roster of the great men of America. Eight had been signers of the Declaration of Independence. Others had risked all in the war. Washington was chosen as chairman, a popular choice; he would talk little and act with justice.

As the convention went on, Edmund Randolph read a list of fifteen suggestions. He called them "the Virginia plan." These ideas were not accepted, but they gave the delegates something definite to consider.

Soon men saw that they could agree on a few points:

The Articles must be disregarded, not just patched up.

The new government must have three parts; legislative, judicial, and executive, each with carefully balanced powers.

State governments must consider the good of all people. Old debts must be paid.

Congress must control interstate commerce, common defense, and the welfare of the people.

So far so well; but how to do this was quite another matter, and men had wide differences of opinion. It really was not easy because the United States were only a group of states joined together for the common good; they were not actually a nation. Men like Hamilton wanted a strong federal government; they were called "Federalists." Others, like Jefferson, wanted to keep the states strong so that there could never be a powerful central government, controlling the country. They were called "Republicans" because they favored a republic of states. Fine, loyal men were on both sides of the vigorous debates.

May turned to June. July came, with hot humid days that were no help to frayed tempers. Washington almost despaired. Madison worked desperately to keep the convention going. At the end of July a committee was appointed to work on details, and the convention adjourned for nine days—a needed respite.

Washington, with Robert Morris and a few others, went out to Valley Forge to fish. He could hardly recognize the place. As he climbed hills and strolled over meadows, he saw that strong young trees had grown tall enough to hide the old stumps and the fallen huts. As he tried to identify this place and that, a cheering thought came to him; some day a new America would grow up with new strength. In time, old disagreements, like the rotting stumps, would be forgotten by a vigorous new nation.

The next day Washington caught some perch, learned a new way to plant buckwheat, and felt better. The convention went better, too, when it convened again.

By September, a compromise plan was approved. Thirty-nine delegates signed it. Those men well knew that the Constitution was not perfect. But they had done their best.

In time this Constitution came to be regarded as one of the important steps in man's climb to freedom. The first three words, "We the people . . ." had a special meaning in that document; it meant all the people: rich, poor, educated, ignorant—everyone in the country. The Constitution said that "We the people" intend to govern ourselves—a privilege and a responsibility.

When the Constitution was signed and printed, people got it and read it eagerly. Some understood the meaning better than others but the reading helped all people to know what their country was trying to be. Many were so proud that they framed the printed words and hung them in a place of honor.

When the work of the convention ended, Washington wanted to hurry home. But he had promised Dr. Franklin he would call and see a new invention—an ironing machine he called a "mangle."

Washington admired the ingenious machine and noted that it was good for ironing "tablecloths and such articles as have not plaits . . . and would be useful in large families." Later he bought a mangle for Mount Vernon. Then he did some personal business, bade his kind hosts, the Morrises, good-by, and left for home.

He soon found that his work for the Constitution was only begun. Two thirds of the states must ratify it, that is, accept it by vote, before it could become legal. People argued for and against it; they saw the advantage of union but each loved his own state and feared a strong central government.

Washington, at Mount Vernon, wrote hundreds of letters, all in long hand, of course. He explained the Constitution and urged people to accept it. He and his secretary, Tobias Lear, got a new-style letter press, an ingenious thing for keeping a record of letters sent out. A freshly written page was put under tissue with a piece of thin dampened linen on top and an imprint was made in a press. The tissue copies were later bound into letter books. In after years these books were found and they showed exactly what Washington had written.

Newspapers and patriots argued for or against the Constitution, according to their convictions. Perhaps the most important work for that document was written by James Madison, John Jay, and Alexander Hamilton. They wrote a series of papers which they published anonymously. Later the papers were put into a book called *The Federalist,* and the authors' identities became known.

Each state was to call a special convention to vote for the Constitution, and as these conventions met, people over the country watched eagerly to see how the vote went. Delaware, New Jersey, and Pennsylvania ratified in December; Georgia and Connecticut in January, 1788; Massachusetts in February; South Carolina in May. Now eight states had agreed to live under government by this constitution—nine were needed to make it legal.

Where was Virginia? Washington was worried—and chagrined. He had hoped that Virginia would be among the first! In June he went up to Alexandria to be closer to news, and word came that New Hampshire had ratified! The town on the Potomac rejoiced when four days later word came that Virginia had ratified. Townspeople paraded and feasted. Washington attended a dinner party in celebration. (New York ratified in July, North Carolina in November, and Rhode Island in May, 1790.)

But the states did not need to wait for the final three; they made plans for an electoral college to chose the president. There were no political parties then, nor pledging of delegates. The electors met, and each delegate voted for his own choice. Naturally there was talk about who would be chosen.

"I see one man is to be the head of everything," a man would say, a bit anxiously. No one wanted a king. "Who would they get to be president? It's a big thing for one man."

"George Washington is my choice," was a frequent reply. "He's a great man but he doesn't put on airs."

"Seems like I trust that man," someone was sure to remark.

Patriots came to Mount Vernon and talked with Washington. But he gave them no encouragement.

"I spoke truly," he said to them, "when I resigned from the army. I wish to stay in retirement, here in Mount Vernon." Some waylaid Martha and asked her to persuade him, but she gave them no satisfaction. Why should she want to leave home?

In January of 1789 the states voted for their electors, and a month later these men met and unanimously elected George Washington as the first president of the United States of America. This man they chose was not a lawyer, nor an orator, but he had qualities the people wanted in their government. He believed in the new republic and was faithful to it; he was honest, just, and people trusted him.

The old Congress was to meet and as its last act, make the election official. Ice and storms prevented travel; they could not meet until April. Then, the vote taken, a messenger was sent to Mount Vernon to tell the general.

"They want you to come at once, General," the man said.

"I shall need three days ... then I shall leave." When all the people wanted him, he could not refuse.

As Washington rode over the fields with his nephew-manager, George Augustine Washington, he thought of plans for new crops, ideas for further improving the house and grounds, and all the delightful things he meant to do. His patriotism almost failed him; he wanted so much to stay.

But he enjoyed public service, too. He stiffened his shoulders and made plans for a long absence. On the third day he was happy, almost gay when, everything attended to, he rode off toward Alexandria and new responsibilities.

Nelly and George Custis, now ten and eight years old, clung to Martha as the men rode through the big west gate. Somehow they knew that this was no ordinary leaving.

When the travelers were out of sight, Martha straightened her shoulders and became her usual brisk self.

"Now then," she said, "we must pack, too. The general wants us with him in New York. Go straight and finish your practicing, Nelly!"

Mr. President

Before he left for New York, Washington went to Fredericksburg to visit his mother. Betty and George had persuaded her, years before, to move into town, and George had purchased for her an attractive white frame house near Kenmore, Betty's home. A wide porch at the back looked over a garden—Mrs. Washington loved gardening—and a box-bordered walk led to Betty's door. As long as her health was good, Mary Washington led an active life, visiting the farm, walking about town, and enjoying Betty's children. But this year, 1789, she was eighty years old—and ill.

During the years that Washington was a burgess at Williamsburg, he stopped often in Fredericksburg to visit his mother. But that service had ended in 1774.

The two sat in comfortable chairs by the cheerful fireplace, and he told her of his new work and honors. What did she think as she looked across at this tall, serious man, her eldest son? He was always getting into danger! She had worried endlessly about battles—yet here he was, the first president of a new country. Washington's glance must have been caught by the great tester bed which had been brought down to this room. It was a cherished thing; his mother was always proud

of it. But the fact that it was there, downstairs, was evidence
of her failing strength. Both knew this was their last meeting.

The old Congress had chosen New York City as the seat
of the government. Washington had expected to make a quiet,
rapid journey to his new task. To his astonishment, festivities
all along the way slowed his travel. The tour became a personal
triumph that might have turned the head of a lesser man.
Every town and village had its cheering crowd.

At Gray's Ferry over the Schuylkill, an arch of laurel was
erected over the street. Flags of the thirteen states waved gaily.
Banners with slogans read: "Don't tread on me!" "The New
Era," "The Rising Empire." Boats literally covered the river.
Newspapers reported that twenty thousand people lined the
road to Philadelphia. "Long live Washington!" people shouted.

"Long live the father of his people!"

Near Trenton—where Washington had crossed in 1776—
a triumphal arch twenty feet wide was erected. Thirteen col-
umns were twined with evergreen and topped with a huge
floral design, which said, "To you alone!" Women and girls,
dressed in white, sang,

> "Welcome, mighty chief, once more
> Welcome to the grateful shore.
> Now no mercenary foe
> Aims again the fatal blow."

The last verse ended with the line, "Strew our hero's way
with flowers." At these words flowers were tossed onto the road.

People packed the street, hung from windows, and sat
on roofs to witness the inaugural on the balcony of
Federal Hall. They would never forget it.

At Elizabethtown the party, now considerably larger than when it started at Mount Vernon, boarded a barge for New York. Thirteen masters of vessels, wearing fancy fringed caps, rowed the barge across the river. Guns boomed. So many boats crowded near, that steering was quite a feat. Crowds cheered themselves hoarse. Hats tossed high blew into the river, and a school of curious porpoises swam near to see what the fuss was about. They made navigation still more difficult.

Washington stood where he was told to place himself and bowed and bowed. No one knew what he was thinking about this display. When he left home, he, the man rich in acres, had stopped in Alexandria to borrow cash for this journey and his immediate expenses in New York. Farmers would understand that spring was not the time to catch a farmer in funds!

But when the people sang new words to the tune "God Save The King," and guns on a Spanish ship boomed in salute, he understood what the people cheered. They were proud of the new government that he represented.

Landing at New York was difficult, for the wharf was jammed with people. Troops had to clear the way. And finally Washington and his party walked the half mile to Franklin House, where there was a reception.

April thirtieth was chosen for the inauguration, and every inn and lodging house in town was full for a fortnight. New York people liked a spectacle; they would put it on well, though not everyone approved the fuss.

"Too much like a king," some remarked, annoyed.

People wondered what Washington should be called—
"Your Excellency?" "Your Highness?" "Sir?" or what? Congress chose "The President of the United States," with "Mr.
President" as the form of direct address.

Early on the thirtieth, guns boomed from Fort Washington. Church bells began at nine and rang out half an hour
before special services. At noon troops marched to escort the
President-elect, and half an hour later, the parade was moving
toward Federal Hall. This building on Wall Street, by Broadway, had been the City Hall. When the old Congress had
chosen to meet in New York, the building was spruced up
and renamed. Washington was escorted to the Senate Room
and then to the balcony outside, where he was to take the oath
of office.

People packed the street, hung from windows and balanced
precariously on roofs to witness that scene on the balcony of
Federal Hall. They would never forget it: a table draped with
crimson velvet, a Bible on a velvet cushion; a tall, handsome
dignified man dressed in a dark-brown American-made cloth
suit with metal buttons each imprinted with an eagle, white
silk stockings, plain silver shoebuckles, a dress sword, and hair
powdered in the fashion of the day. Few noticed the others
on that small balcony. All eyes were fixed on one man. Cheers
were hushed while, for the first time, a president said:

"I do solemnly swear . . . that I will faithfully execute the
office of President of the United States and will to the best of
my ability, preserve, protect and defend the Constitution of the

United States." Washington had seen that Constitution grow from its beginning. He had said it was the best that could be evolved from many minds. The country could trust him to defend it.

Guns boomed, telling people all over the city that they had a president. Cheers were deafening. People scattered as the President went inside to give his short inaugural address. This was the worst ordeal of the day for Washington, but he got through with it. Then the President, Vice-President John Adams, and all the legislators walked to special services at Saint Paul's Church.

The celebration lasted through the evening. Hundreds of houses had gay "illuminated windows" (transparent pictures with a light behind) in the new fashion. "Italian candles" lighted the sky with multicolored balls of fire. "Set-pieces" showed pictures or slogans in fire.

Washington watched the bright scene from Mr. Livingston's house, and then called his coach to drive home. But the great coach could not move even one block through the mass of people; so, quietly, the President slipped out and walked to his room.

The next morning Washington began the business of the new government.

There was a bewildering lot for the President, with the help of the Vice-President, to do. He must form a cabinet, make appointments, meet callers, write letters, and set up a household of his own. In the midst of everything he advertised for a cook and a coachman. Martha and the children came to join him, but New York ways were new to her, too.

One of the difficulties was that there was nothing to go by—no precedent. Washington couldn't ask, "What was done before?" because there had never before been a president elected by a free people. He felt he must be cautious, because later people would say, "This is the way it used to be done." He understood the value of precedents and wanted to establish good ones. Especially, he wanted people to feel free to come and talk to him.

Soon he found that if he listened to every visitor he would have no time for anything else. He had to set visiting hours to limit his own social life. Some said he was being haughty, but he was never that; he was simply trying to get his work done.

The selection of men to serve on his cabinet was one of the President's first important duties. He chose Thomas Jefferson to be Secretary of State; Jefferson was in France just then but would return home soon. He chose Henry Knox as Secretary of War and Alexander Hamilton as Secretary of the Treasury. Edmund Randolph was his choice for Attorney General, the president's lawyer. John Jay was asked to be Chief Justice of the Supreme Court. These men were honest patriots; Washington was pleased when they accepted.

Gradually, not in one year or even in two, the United States government came to be a going concern. The President was a good administrator; he had a gift for picking men, and was willing to listen patiently to many opinions.

But the heavy program and the confining work began to affect his health. He missed the long rides over his plantation, the out of doors, the informal visiting with friends. As the days warmed he had a severe illness. In August his mother died. That year of 1789 was too full of honors, troubles, and duties for one man's strength. Friends urged him to take a respite from work.

So for a diversion, he took a journey by coach through parts of New England. But he was back in time to work on his message to Congress after the new year.

This message was written, of course, in the formal, stilted style of Washington's time. But its content was shrewd and idealistic. He appealed for national strength for self-defense, and gave his reasons. Spain, with the Floridas and the Mississippi Valley, controlled thousands of Indians. Britain was growing stronger to the northwest. Settlers who ventured into the vast middle west needed a strong nation behind them. But the states that were united were only a slender strip along the coast. "Providing for common defense will merit particular regard," he said.

"To be prepared for war," Washington continued, "is one of the most effective means of preserving peace. A free people not only ought to be armed but disciplined . . . a uniform plan is requisite." He said that the country needed a military school, better relations with the Indians, and peace with other nations. He asked for a standard of weights and measures and a uniform currency; good naturalization laws; help for agriculture, commerce and industry; and a national university. The message considered the entire country.

In the spring of 1790 Washington felt that the new government was beginning to work quite well. Perhaps he could take a vacation. His journey to New England had pleased people, so he decided he would visit in southern states. He went to the Carolinas and to Virginia and enjoyed meeting and talking with new friends he made on the trip.

Late that same year Congress decided to move the seat of government to Philadelphia for ten years. This act gave pleasure to the President; Philadelphia was a second home to him. Most of his civilian work for the country had been done there; he had often been there on war duties; and the city was nearer Mount Vernon than New York.

Meanwhile, during those ten years, Congress expected to build a new city for the permanent use of the government. Maryland and Virginia gave land, ten square miles in all, on the banks of the Potomac. This location was felt to be a good choice; the place was between the north and the south and the city would be newly built expressly for the government.

Washington knew the location well; low land on the river, convenient for boat transport, with hills around for beautiful vistas. He determined that the design of that city and its buildings should be beautiful, worthy of the ideals of the new nation. After careful study he appointed Pierre Charles L'Enfant, a trained city planner, to lay out the new project. For the present it was called The Federal City.

Other changes, besides moving the government to Philadelphia, were taking place. When Washington was elected president, there were no political parties. During the war, people who favored the British king were called Tories and those who supported the war were Whigs. But after the war, most Tories moved to Canada or to England. Americans were no longer Whigs in the old sense, they all voted with the new government--but they had different ideas about how their country should be managed.

Washington had chosen men of various ideas for his cabinet—Hamilton and Jefferson, for instance—because he wanted to be fair to all. But the cabinet meetings became scenes of such violent debates that only a man like the President could have kept the government working.

Hamilton and Jefferson were brilliant, honest men and devoted to their country. But they differed widely about how to manage government business.

By the beginning of Washington's fourth year in office, the controversy between those two men grew more intense. The President was worried and anxious and many a night looked forward to the peace of Mount Vernon.

"But you must serve again, Mr. President!" men exclaimed, when he spoke of being through with his work. "It is because there are such disputes that you must stay."

Reluctantly, Washington consented to lay aside his wishes.

"If it should happen that the people want me," he said to a friend, "I shall serve." But he hoped he would not be called.

Washington Steps Aside

Washington was unanimously re-elected to the presidency, and in the spring of 1793, he took the oath without any fanfare. It was an ominous time in world history.

At home, the cabinet was seriously divided about methods of managing the country's business. Indian troubles endangered settlers in the middle west. Abroad, France was in the turmoil of revolution. Louis XVI, who had befriended America, had been beheaded in January. France seemed about to declare war upon England. Perhaps all of Europe would be involved. France was sure to ask for help. What should the United States do?

Washington was in a difficult position. Most Americans liked France and remembered gratefully her help in their own hard fight. And there was the treaty signed in 1778 which had brought the American patriots men and arms.

On April the nineteenth the President called a cabinet meeting to study the problem of aid to France. Members thoughtfully pondered every side of the question. Jefferson knew France well; he had represented the United States there. Cabinet men could not forget their joy and relief when French arms arrived in time of need. But what could a new nation, barely functioning and burdened with debt, actually do? Suppose they tried to help and failed? The whole dream of a free country in the new world would be lost. The little, the very little they could do was surely not worth risking that disaster.

The consultations lasted a long time. In the end it was decided that the United States should be neutral in all European conflicts. The principle established then was followed for many years. Later Washington thought that the country needed a better understanding with Britain. British troops were still in the West. He sent John Jay to London to work out a settlement. The treaty he framed was ratified by Congress in 1795.

Early in Washington's second term, Thomas Jefferson withdrew from the cabinet. By this time, shades of political opinion had grown into serious differences. Two parties, two ways of looking at national needs, were evolving. As many saw it, the main point was whether the country wished to be a nation, strong in federal control, or a republic, a union of states, as the Constitution had planned.

Alexander Hamilton believed in a strong federal government; through his skillful work, war debts had been paid at par, the country's credit had been established, and there was a sound national bank. These were remarkable achievements, and the country prospered. People who believed as he did called themselves Federalists.

Thomas Jefferson believed in people more, perhaps, than Hamilton did. He disapproved of some of Hamilton's successes, especially the national bank. Jefferson did not want strong federal power. He thought of the nation as a republic, a group of states working together; he wanted the states to have power over as much as possible of the country's business. People who believed as he did called themselves Anti-Federalists; they were republicans. Citizens began to choose between parties according to their own opinions.

The three great political events of Washington's second term were the creating of a national bank, the declaration of American neutrality, and the rise of two parties.

Washington's health had been fine in 1787 when he went to the Constitutional Convention, but he was never so well again. Artists who came to paint the President found him looking weary. His lips were set tight; his expression stern.

It was true that the President was tired. But the stern look was caused by constant trouble with the teeth of rhinoceros ivory, which were the best dentists could make for him. The things were held together with a spring and had to be kept in place by his tongue. He never knew, at a dinner party or even in a meeting, when they might give a terrible pinch to the inside of his cheek. And the artists wanted him to look pleasant!

"Smile, Mr. President!" they coaxed. Public life did have its troubles!

Time went on and rumors about a third term reached the President. He decided to say his "No" promptly. People would then have plenty of time to decide upon a successor. It seemed vain to decline when he was not yet chosen, so he planned to put his refusal in the form of a "Farewell Address" to the nation. He could speak his views in such a message and make clear at the same time that he was stepping aside.

Toward the end of his first term, he had begun such a paper. He had talked with James Madison about what should go into it. Washington hunted out the four-year-old paper and reread it. Madison was thinking more like Jefferson these days. Washington had changed some of his own ideas, he found. He worked on the paper, and then handed it to Madison.

"See what you make of it and let me know," he said. "I want the ideas stated simply. You have more writing ability than I have. Make it as clear as you can."

When Madison returned the paper, Washington gave it to Hamilton. He still believed that all sides of a question should be considered. Hamilton rewrote it. Then Washington worked on it and gave it to John Jay for his opinion.

Finally, Washington rewrote the whole message in his own hand, altering, smoothing, putting in commas. The paper was entitled "Washington's Farewell Address," and was published in September of 1796. This was well before the date when voters must choose electors for the next presidential election.

In the address Washington discussed three main topics that he thought important to the new nation:

He begged for loyalty to the Union. "Unity of government . . . is your real independence . . . your very Liberty."

He asked citizens to work for harmony throughout the nation. "Virtue and Morality (are the) . . . necessary spring of popular government."

He advised against partiality among nations and asked for "Good faith and justice to all . . . peace and harmony with all."

The message had a fatherly tone and he called his words the "counsels of an old and affectionate friend." Washington was seeing his work for his country as finished.

Federalists liked the address better than did the Anti-Federalists. But in time people of various shades of political opinion cherished it because it summed up Washington's honest views after his many years of faithful service to his country.

Another March fourth came, this time in the year 1797. John Adams was the newly elected President of the United States and Thomas Jefferson was the Vice-President. George Washington stood at one side in the historic room in Independence Hall in Philadelphia and watched the new President take the oath of office.

A great relief swept over Washington as he realized that his time of service was ended. Under President Adams, government would be different; that was to be expected in a free country. It was even a good thing: it made people think. The habits of government were now strong enough, he was sure, to stand the strains of discussion and change.

People crowded on the streets to catch a glimpse of the retiring President. To many, Washington seemed to be a symbol of American government: the man whose strength and upright character had guided the country through its early troubles.

A few days later, Mr. and Mrs. Washington with Nelly and George Washington Parke Custis left for Mount Vernon. With every mile of the journey, Washington felt the load lighten. Each time he had returned for a vacation, he loved this home more. Now he hoped to stay there for the rest of his life. Young people, his loved nieces and nephews, would come to see him. He would ride for hours over the plantation and plan new work. There were many pleasures awaiting him.

Probably what comes is never quite what is expected. As he rode south on that happy day, Washington did not think of the many visitors he was to have, some friendly, others curious and demanding. He did not know that his country would call again, asking him to raise an army to fight against France. Happily President Adams made a peace and avoided that misery for him.

Nor did he know of some pleasures, either. One was a visit from Lafayette's son, George Washington Lafayette, an attractive young man. But perhaps the event that gave Washington the greatest pleasure was a wedding.

Mount Vernon was a popular gathering place for nieces and nephews and their friends and among the most constant visitors was Washington's nephew Lawrence, Betty's son. The general was pleased but hardly surprised when Lawrence appeared at his study and asked to marry Nelly Custis.

"We are going to be married on your birthday, Grandfather," Nelly announced. She kissed him and smiled as he flushed with pleasure.

At twilight on that February day a houseman went about with a taper, lighting lamps and candles. Fires crackled and glowed. Branches of pine and box scented the rooms and mirrors reflected twinkling lights, lace-ruffled coats and gowns of many hues.

Washington went to the study for a bit of quiet before the guests arrived. As often, he stood before Lawrence's portrait; perhaps on this day he remembered Lawrence's wedding. Then his eye caught the framed commission of 1740. War had seemed a glorious adventure, then.

"How young I was!" he thought, half amused, and went to the hall to greet his guests.

Suddenly he missed the Fairfaxes; they always liked a party. George William and Sally had gone to London twenty-five years ago and had never returned. Washington himself had been away sixteen years of that time—eight for the war, eight for the presidency. Yet he still missed these friends.

But this was no time for sadness. Another coach arrived and young people from Alexandria poured into the hall, laughing, teasing him because now his granddaughter would be his niece.

Soon tones of harpsichord and violin hushed the laughter and Washington stepped to the foot of the stairway to meet Nelly. She never looked so beautiful, he thought, as slowly, her head high, she came down the stairs to take his hand.

Together they entered the drawing room for the ceremony.

Washington let the groom have the first dance; then he bowed to Nelly.

"May I have the honor, Mrs. Lewis?" he said. His eyes twinkled as she looked at him, startled, in the way of brides, to hear her new name.

"Indeed you may—General!" Nelly laughed as she took his arm. "I dare not call you Grandfather tonight, for you look as young as the next one!" It was one of the happiest days of his life.

Spring came, then summer; and each year the mansion and grounds grew more beautiful. Espaliered fruits thrived around the herb garden. Locust trees dripped with fragrant bloom. Autumn turned the dogwood scarlet; maples were gold and crimson and the scent of boxwood drifted over the garden.

On a December day Washington rode about his farms as usual. A wet snow dampened his clothing, but he was not concerned.

"My greatcoat protected me," he said to Martha when she begged him to change before sitting down to dinner. The day went on as usual with reading, writing, and talk; by evening he felt weary and his throat hurt.

In the night his illness grew worse. At daylight messengers dashed off for doctors. Three came; one was the old friend, Dr. Craik, of Alexandria. But the drastic remedies of the times weakened instead of helped the sick man. He died on the fourteenth day of December.

Word did not reach Congress until the day of the funeral. They could hardly believe it. On the nineteenth confirmation came to President Adams; Washington had died and was buried on the grounds at Mount Vernon. The next day announcement was formally made in the House of Representatives by John Marshall, and after a resolution of respect, Congress adjourned.

On December twenty-sixth, a memorial meeting was addressed by Major General Henry Lee. Too often such speeches are forgotten but the final phrases of Lee's stirring address have lived through the many years. He said of George Washington: "First in war, first in peace, and first in the hearts of his countrymen, he was second to none in the humble and endearing scenes of private life."

As time went on, traditions about George Washington flourished like the trees at Valley Forge, hiding the real man. Hero-tales made him perfect, set apart. It was all but forgotten that he was a man of the soil, and very human.

He was born a Virginia aristocrat. Yet when he had the whole army to choose from his best friends were a Connecticut farmer, a Boston bookseller, and a young man from the West Indies who had neither fortune nor family. Somehow, people from all walks of life believed in him. He seemed like a rock in a time when all else was shifting sand. Perhaps this was because he had a deep sense of responsibility and his great qualities were steadiness and honesty.

And always George Washington was a gentleman, considerate of others, thoughtful, and courteous. He was at ease anywhere, in the settler's cabin, in the wilderness, at the head of an army, in the President's chair. Wherever he was, he commanded respect because he so lived that he could respect himself.

On the twenty-first of February, 1885, crowds of people gathered in the city of Washington to dedicate a monument built in memory of their first President. The lofty spire of masonry, tallest in the world, soared heavenward like a dream. It had been years in building, but it was strong. It would last a long time.

The man whose life that spire symbolized had a high ideal for the new republic, so high that it might not be achieved in one century or two. But progress toward his lofty goal would go steadily forward as long as men were willing to lay aside personal ambition as he did, and serve their country. Today, as in his time, a land that would be free needs faithful men of high ideals and integrity—men like George Washington.